Japan Is Very Wonderful

The Guide to Tokyo, Hakone, Kyoto and the Kumano Kodo by Pearl Howie

First Edition
Copyright © Pearl Howie 2017
Published by Pearl Escapes
All rights reserved
ISBN 978-0-9956474-1-1
The moral right of the author has been asserted

I believe that people (and books and places and jobs and many other things) come into your life for a reason, a season or a lifetime.

So this is for the people in my life who came for a reason or a season – thank you for being there and thank you for helping me to let go.

(Oh, and for Sally, of course, for introducing me to sushi and for not constantly bringing up my attempt to eat raw octopus.)

Contents

Introduction	6
Japan in December	13
About Our Trip to Japan	14
The Hotel – Hotel Chinzanso Tokyo	16
The Spa – Hotel Chinzanso Tokyo	19
The Restaurant – Il Teatro – Hotel Chinzanso Tokyo	21
The Sight - Tokyo – Meiji Jingu Shrine	24
Train from Tokyo to Hakone (Odawara Station)	27
The Ryokan (Hotel, Spa and Restaurant) – KAI Hakone	28

The Sight – Hakone – Mount Fuji from Lake Ashi	45
Train from Hakone (Odawara Station) to Kyoto	48
The Hotel – Kyoto – Screen	49
The Massage – Kyoto – Room Service at Screen	53
The Sight – Kyoto - Fushimi Inari Shrine	54
The Massage – Kyoto – Anma at Asahido Massage Therapy Clinic	61
The Sight – Kyoto - Night Time at Tenryuji Temple	64
The Restaurant – Kyoto – Room Service at Screen and a Few More Food and Drink Tips	68
Train from Kyoto to Wakayama	70
The Hotel – Granvia Wakayama	72
The Sight – Nachi Falls and the Daimon-zaka on the Kumano Kodo	74
Train from Wakayama to Osaka	90
The Sight – Osaka Castle and The Santa Orchestra	91
Osaka - Hotel New Otani (or New Hotel Otani)	92
The Spa and Massage – Osaka – New Hotel Otani	94
The Restaurant - New Otani Osaka	95
The Flight	97
Onsen (Japanese Hot Spring) - Etiquette and Practice	98
The Rest	101
Photo Credits	109
About the Author	109
Other Titles by the Author	110

Introduction

I didn't want to go to Japan. I mean it wasn't my pick, for the first time I was organising a trip for a client. I was going too, but it was their dream, their once in a lifetime and so, as well as listening to my heart, my intuition, I was trying to listen closely and pick up on their vibe - what was their escape in Japan?

It worked.

Finally we found the perfect escape for her in Japan, or rather she found it when I left her alone. Because leaving her alone was the best gift I could give.

I'd like to think it was the magnificent shrines, the sublime massages, the incredibly kind and helpful people, the quirky and other worldly hotels, and of course, the food, oh the food…

Japanese food is actually listed as a Unesco World Heritage… thing. With good reason, their train station sushi is better than almost any sushi I've tried outside Japan. Their kaiseki dinners look on paper and in photos designed as a kind of culinary assault course but the one we had in Hakone was the most perfect blend of flavours, textures and most importantly chemicals, yes, chemicals, acidity and alkalinity that I felt healthier with each course. And all of it, yes all of it, is served - not just the food, but the spaces, the hotel bills, your shopping, even nature itself, all of it is served elegantly, beautifully. I have never experienced such reverence for beauty, as if a lack of beauty is unnecessary. Most of all I have never experienced such a reverence for nature.

So yes, I think it all came together. I'd like to think so, I like to think I helped her find the magic of Japan, to find her perfect escape.   It certainly seemed so at the time.

First there was the insomnia, initially jet lag, which carried on for weeks back in England. Luckily over Christmas I was staying in a hotel on the seafront so had some memorable moonlit and sunrise walks, over New Year I was in an incredible country spa in Essex where the pool opened so early I could watch the sunrise from the hot tub. (Put like that insomnia, and early rising sound more like a gift, which I guess they are.)

Although I was soon back to normal, waking early came back with a vengeance on my next trip to Arizona, and then even more powerfully back home, where after twenty years I discovered full moons and sunrises from odd vantage points I'd never appreciated.

Japan's nature, which I felt was talking to me at times, waking me up, also awakened me to nature in Arizona, nature all around my bedroom, as well as to my own nature and my deep need to be outside, near trees, climbing trees, hugging trees. .. which doesn't seem so strange when I remember the shrine near Nachi Falls - the real shrine; not the building but the wizened, magical ancient tree that was worshipped as well as the waterfall in the Shinto tradition.

In Japan nature was talking so loudly to me I actually started to listen.

Then there was the tidying.

We were spoilt in most of the hotels with vast spaces (going against the theory that Japan has the smallest hotel rooms in the world) …and they were gorgeous.
My favourite was my room in Kyoto.

The elegance of the Japanese hotels made me feel so happy. It also made me feel like a gargantuan hick, like a cowboy walking into The Ritz, but hey.

I'd left my flat with no thought two weeks before Christmas, having treated it as I'd become used to – like a staging area for my classes, and my Christmas party. I'd washed a mountain of clothes and flung them around to dry, or at least make my flat smell mouldy.

So I opened my door. Halfway. Because there was something behind it stopping it opening. I had no idea how ignorant I'd become to my surroundings.

In my Christmas and New Year hotels I kept my room beautifully tidy, whilst also reading Marie Kondo's book on Tidying Up.

By the end of January 2016 I had binned, donated or given away half of all my possessions. Magically everything I kept fit perfectly into the space I already had in my cupboards. I had never needed a bigger house, just less stuff. I painted my kitchen pink, painted the sky on my walls to let nature in, rearranged the furniture, put my white obi belt from Japan on the table and had a new flat. In the next seven months I bought only two items of clothing, neither of which I really needed, saved hours on finding stuff (especially socks) and put my flat on the market without having to do a massive clear out. …and I realise I still have way more than I need. It's been a massive shift, from thinking more, more, more to less, less, less. It's given me freedom to enjoy my flat, open the front door and to spend way more time outside, away from the house and housework, in nature.

The night before I left for Japan I watched a programme I love ("Grey's Anatomy"). In that episode one of the main characters died, the love of the life of another main character, which really affected me. (I know, it's only a TV show, but sometimes when you see something onscreen it triggers something.) Standing at Nachi Falls, the highest waterfall in Japan, which is worshipped as a goddess in the Shinto tradition, I accepted for the first time that my ex was the love of my life, however broken that relationship seemed to be. Accepting that, taking those next steps, opening up again, sharing ideas and stories, hopes and dreams with him enabled me to understand not only my own life, my own reactions and habits but also come to a deeper understanding of life, love and the drama that we keep inviting into that sacred space.

Whatever happens now happens without blame or anger, just peace, unconditional love and a deeper understanding than I ever thought I would have of all relationship struggles.

So thank you Japan. I thought I knew something of you when I planned this trip, I've read so many books about China and read how those authors perceived Japan, there are dark echoes from World War II, I watched movies set in and about Japan, been to Japanese restaurants, seen Japanese cartoons, met a few Japanese people…

…nothing prepared me for how kind, how clean, how helpful, how beautiful, how dedicated, how efficient, how funny, how magical, how sweet, how delicious Japan would actually be.

Japan is very wonderful.

Japan in December

See the shadowed mountains of the Kumano Kodo as the sun rises like a ball of fire.

Bathe naked in Japanese onsen.

Learn how to wear traditional Japanese yukata and slippers.

Enjoy the elaborate perfection of a kaiseki dinner of around 10 courses (some with 9 or 10 morsels).

Climb through thousands of red torii gates to the top of Mount Inari.

Walk through moon and lantern lit bamboo forests around a temple in Kyoto.

Enjoy traditional Japanese massage in pyjamas.

Hug eight hundred year old trees on the Daimon-zaka as you climb to Nachi Falls.

Visit Japanese gardens with pagodas, waterfalls and koi where the autumn has tinted the leaves red and gold.

Stay in a hotel that boasts not only its own official Santa Claus but 12 restaurants, bars, a hair salon, a shopping mall, an onsen, a spa, two chapels, its own dentist and a medical facility (there was probably more but we were a bit tired by then) overlooking Osaka Castle.

About Our Trip to Japan

It's my belief that far from being "just a room" your hotel is your base. Sometimes all you need is a hot shower or a place to lay your head, but because we were visiting a very different culture I wanted hotels that would steer us through any miscommunication, not Western chain hotels but hotels that appeared to cater to Western customers. Looking at the places I'm recommending I realise how lazy a lot of it seems now; so often the restaurant, the spa, even the sight were right there in the hotel. Part of this was in the planning, part in good luck, but I think this is also part of the Japanese culture. Our massage at Screen Hotel in Kyoto wasn't on the menu, I just had a feeling, as in China or even Florida that massage might be something so fundamental that the hotel wouldn't bat an eyelid at organizing one in room (and they didn't). These hotels all did such a fantastic job of bringing the best to us, their guests, that even when we did venture outside it was hard to top what our hosts had sourced.

When confused I follow simple rules; follow my heart, find a great hotel (that makes my heart beat a little faster) where or with what I want and then always, always ask their advice.

The sights in Tokyo, Hakone, Kyoto (night time temple) and shopping in Osaka were all a result of helpful concierges. Although people were so helpful everywhere that chances are you'd get the same advice asking your host in a simple ryokan or a guy at the bus stop. The one experience I really can take credit for is the Kumano Kodo and Nachi Falls sight which was fuelled by slightly inaccurate magazine articles, websites, local information and finally brought together pushing through reluctance from the receptionist in booking such an expensive taxi. When I visited China I was surprised by how much harder it was than I'd anticipated, in Japan it was the opposite, it felt like the country was bending over backwards to make everything as easy and comfortable as possible.

Approximately £2,500 per person including all hotels, trains, planes, taxis, food, sights… everything. (Two nights Tokyo, one night Hakone, two nights Kyoto, two nights Wakayama and one night Osaka.)

For the latest transport options and costs I recommend you check the journey options on www.rome2rio.com (then double check locally – it's not flawless).

Kumano Kodo bus routes are seasonal, most do not run in December, but in the summer you could do a similar route to ours via bus.

The Hotel – Hotel Chinzanso Tokyo

I chose this hotel for its gardens. Japanese gardens were top of my client's list and I believe in going straight to what you want. I also like booking somewhere fabulous with its own highlights for the first night of a trip – that way, if you have a terrible journey or jet lag or are just too fried to leave the hotel you still feel you've arrived, still feel like you're where you wanted to be.

In fact of all the other gardens we visited on this trip, even the wilds of the Kumano Kodo, even the Imperial Gardens (well, the bit we were allowed into), these were the most perfect iconic Japanese gardens, and the autumn colours burst out at us as we arrived. (Also lovely were the little model Christmas scenes displayed around the hotel. They take Christmas very seriously in Japan.)

The gardens had bridges, a waterfall, koi carp, a pagoda, a shrine, restaurants, and much of it was also historic, so this was a fabulous welcome to Japan. We also loved all the wedding groups (Chinzanso Tokyo is a BIG wedding hotel).

The rooms were sumptuous, with spectacular bathrooms; toiletries, robes, even pyjamas in the drawers, a mini-bar, a drawer with more goodies (great for me because I had dreadful jet lag that affected my eating patterns as much as my sleep, so I hacked into some cookies in the middle of the night), plus a tea area with glassware (for your mini bar cocktails), several bottles of complimentary water, lounging area, incredibly comfortable king size bed (I couldn't blame the lack of sleep on that) as well as a whole console of buttons, including blackout curtains (again, couldn't blame the lack of sleep on that).

Service, as you might expect, was flawless, which was nice as we both ordered room service breakfasts (plus, I ordered dinner at 3am after hours of tossing and turning and forgetting that I was in such a world class hotel with a 24 hour kitchen).

The hotel also has a fantastic spa (where I had a continental breakfast overlooking the garden) – more on that in a mo, a ridiculous number of restaurants and its own shopping centre. It also has an "umbrella safe" where you can either borrow or store umbrellas – I've never seen one of these before!

It's worth dressing up in the hotel, especially in the evening, as it is quite elegant. There are also signs warning you not to walk to and from the spa in your robe.

As I mentioned it's a big wedding hotel, so if you're keen to eat in one of the restaurants (and these include top class sushi and other Japanese specialties) do check that these restaurants are not booked out, because we found it very hard to get a table for two people on our first night, despite staying in the hotel.

Facilities: Nine restaurants, garden, spa, shops… it's endless…

Bunkyo-ku, Sekiguchi 2-10-8, Bunkyo Ward, Tokyo, 112-8680
Tel: 813-394-311-11

Narita Express and Skyliner trains run from Narita International Airport. The Narita Express arrives at Ikebukuro Station, 10 minutes away by taxi. The Skyline train arrives at Ueno Station, which is 20 minutes by taxi ride. (We jumped on the train and grabbed a taxi from the station which was very simple as ticket machines are in English and our taxi driver spoke English, although I had a print out of our hotel in Japanese, just in case.)

Premier King Room with City View and Spa Access - Non-Smoking - Single Use £186 per night including taxes but not breakfast. (Superior King £156). Booked via booking.com

The Spa – Hotel Chinzanso Tokyo

Another experience top of my client's (and my) list was a traditional Japanese onsen. This hotel was perfect as I believe it's the only hotel in Tokyo with its own onsen (especially one that transports in local spring water). Although there are many onsen in and around Tokyo, it can be a lot to get into the customs of a local spa, especially if you're just off a long haul flight, so it was perfection to be able to jump in the lift and go straight down to the waters.

Even better, my very first time in a Japanese onsen I was in a great facility with walls of instructions in English, piles of towels, shower caps, anything else I might need and I was alone with five Japanese showers (i.e. with Japanese bathing stools) so I could practise my bathing rituals in private – for more see Onsen (Japanese Hot Spring) - Etiquette and Practice.

This was absolute heaven after being on a plane for so long, not to mention just hitting the "end of term" - finishing teaching my classes (including that full on Christmas party) and needing to let my muscles relax.

The spa is split out as follows; a central welcome area with drinks, where you can also order breakfast, the main swimming pool which has a glass roof, an indoor Jacuzzi with great views of the outdoor waterfall underneath the Japanese maple leaf, a few hot rooms (sauna and steam room) and a wonderfully kitschy Jacuzzi actually outside under the waterfall. (I though this would be my favourite, but the indoor hot tub has a nicer view and the onsen knocked them both out of the running). These facilities are mixed and you will need swimwear.

Then the changing area and separate onsen is single sex, and you MUST NOT wear swimwear in here.

There are also rooms for massages and other treatments. I was more than happy just to partake of the onsen.

N.B. It's really worth noting that for some people a local onsen may be tricky; especially if you have any tattoos. Many onsen apparently do not allow people with tattoos as in Japan they can mean you are part of the Japanese mafia (the Yakuza – not yukata – that's a robe) so, as there was no one to see my tattoos (or lack thereof) this would be a nice way to get around that (some people do put plasters etc. over their tattoos à la Richard Gere in "An Officer and a Gentleman").

The Restaurant – Il Teatro – Hotel Chinzanso Tokyo

Although we struggled to get a table in the hotel (nine restaurants and we weren't sure we were going to be able to eat without getting a taxi into Tokyo central!) we finally bagged a late table at Il Teatro (and then were also offered a table in Le Jardin when we stopped for a pre-dinner cocktail).

Honestly, I am soooo glad we didn't get into the sushi restaurant…

Sometimes it can feel on your first night as if you want to do everything and see everything, but my stomach had been playing up (plane food doesn't help) and this meal was not only one of the most beautifully presented I've ever seen, the most incredibly tasting, it was also one of the healthiest and most balanced. If you see "tofu" or "soy" on a menu and skip over (okay, me too sometimes) this will rock your world and change your mind about healthy eating.

I actually got my best night sleep of the trip the first night, and I think this menu had a lot to do with it.

"Superfood Course

We present the second stage of our exquisite French cuisine course with world-famous nutritious "Super Foods" and ingredients good for your health and beauty, all of which are gluten-free.

Quinoa and chicken breast salad with spirulina, avocado and acai berry sauce served with coconut flavored chia seeds

Apricot and carrot hot smoothie with shrimp, aloe and goji berry

Sautéed Norway salmon with broccoli sprouts, sprouted brown rice with spirulina oil and tomato sauce

Cocoa brownie and soy milk mousse mont blanc

Coffee, tea or herbal tea

(Il Teatro also cooks the room service food.)

6,000 yen per person roughly £33

As at December 2015

The Sight - Tokyo - Meiji Jingu Shrine

We only had one day in Tokyo and our top choice was shopping and checking out the Christmas lights, however they didn't really hold a candle to London or Paris Christmas decorations (although I did love a huge inflatable Raymond Briggs Snowman). So Meiji Jingu, albeit wet, was my favourite sight in Tokyo.

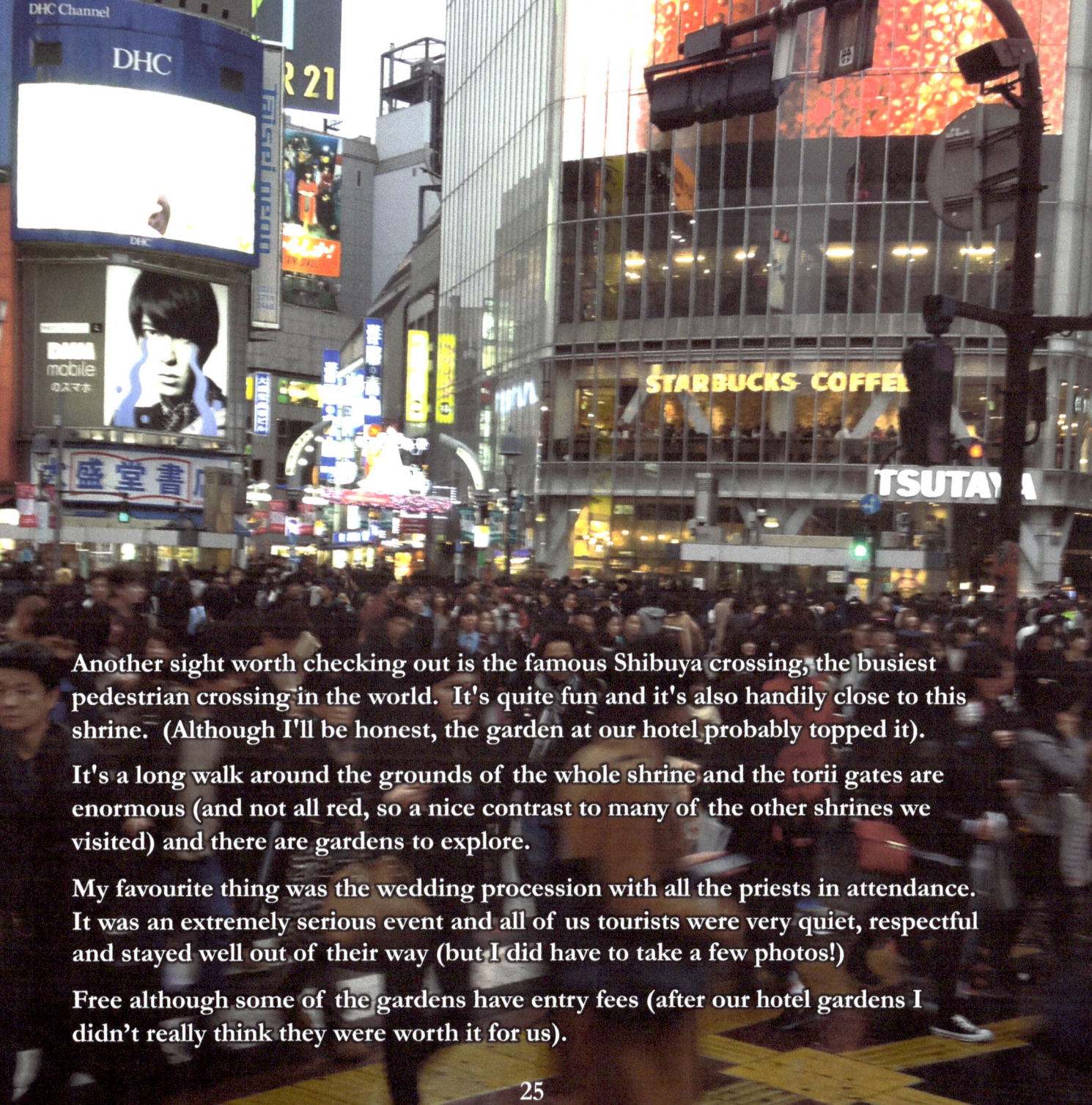

Another sight worth checking out is the famous Shibuya crossing, the busiest pedestrian crossing in the world. It's quite fun and it's also handily close to this shrine. (Although I'll be honest, the garden at our hotel probably topped it).

It's a long walk around the grounds of the whole shrine and the torii gates are enormous (and not all red, so a nice contrast to many of the other shrines we visited) and there are gardens to explore.

My favourite thing was the wedding procession with all the priests in attendance. It was an extremely serious event and all of us tourists were very quiet, respectful and stayed well out of their way (but I did have to take a few photos!)

Free although some of the gardens have entry fees (after our hotel gardens I didn't really think they were worth it for us).

Train from Tokyo to Hakone (Odawara Station)

This was our first shinkansen (bullet train) experience and we were very excited. I also had train station sushi and an iced coffee so was all set.

We headed off, and… it goes so fast, but it's so smooth that it feels just like any other train. Sorry. But it did get us to Hakone in just 35 minutes.

What's really great about the shinkansen is that it has lovely loos and even a Multi-Purpose Room for breastfeeding, changing clothes or for people who just don't feel so good, so it's definitely smooth sailing wherever you want to get to in Japan.

Around £15 plus taxi to our hotel in Hakone.

As at December 2015

The Ryokan (Hotel, Spa and Restaurant) – KAI Hakone

The Hoshino Resorts have been established for over 100 years and I was desperate to stay at least one night in a Hoshino hotel. They describe what they offer as; "Five Spheres of Delight: Hoshinoya flagships – authentic Japan with modern comfort, Risonare – recreation – the art of creating anew, KAI – destinations for blissful bathing and dining, other unique lodgings – getaways with a sense of place, daytrip destinations – thermal soaks and thrilling slopes".

They're spread out all over Japan (and other countries too) but the only one that was open (the Kyoto hotel was being refurbished) anywhere near our path was KAI Hakone.

It wasn't cheap, so I had to juggle our other hotels a little to fit it in the budget. (As a rule Japanese hotels are not that cheap, but now I've experienced Japanese cleanliness and hospitality I wouldn't hesitate to stay in local ryokans with shared bathrooms which are extremely cheap compared to say an average (3 star) US hotel. As many ryokans include dinner and breakfast this makes them an absolute bargain.)

At KAI Hakone our use of the onsen, breakfast and mind blowing kaiseki dinner were all included. But staying here is not just about staying in a glamorous spa hotel with excellent food, what it was, for us, was a brief but effective immersion course in how to be Japanese (or at least understand the rudiments of Japanese culture).

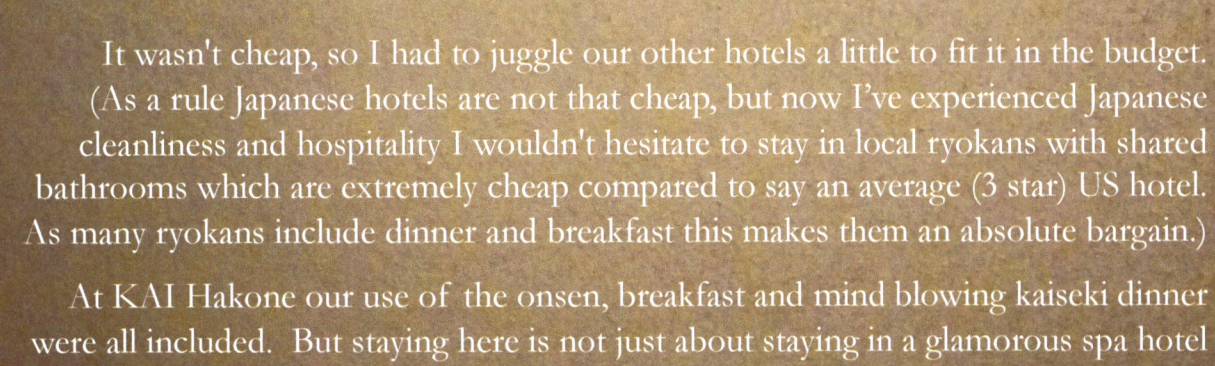

On entering the Japanese house one's shoes are removed, of course, and replaced with slippers. These slippers are worn throughout the room or apartment, even on the tatami mats (which are kept scrupulously clean – no damp towels or dirty clothes please!) then removed in the bathroom and replaced with the toilet slippers.

My Junior Tatami Suite had its own hallway, bathroom, with toiletries and amenities (including a traditional Japanese cloth which is tied into a bag to take to the onsen - my mum really liked it), a separate toilet and rather large shower and tub room with bathing stool, which has the same spring water as in the onsen downstairs.

The hallway continues into the rest of the apartment; a large bedroom, a small kitchenette and an enormous lounge overlooking the brook. With sliding doors between each area you can choose to close everything up or live open wide, with the sound of the brook sending you to sleep. (Unfortunately it had the opposite effect on me.)

Our guide also gave me a tutorial on how to tie my yukata - a light cotton robe. (Some hotels have strict rules on where you can wear your yukata – similar to a spa hotel having rules on where you can wear your robe. At KAI Hakone it is perfectly acceptable to wear your yukata, and the warmer jacket it comes with, to dinner.)

They have a handy English cartoon guide on how to use the onsen which our guide sweetly handed to me. They also have TVs, iPads and other gadgets to play with, but for me, as usual, it was all about the spa (well, until dinner time).

The onsen is downstairs, right on the river, and it's open to the elements, so it's similar to many onsen which are completely open places where healing waters naturally collect. (I realise I have to go back to Japan to visit some of these.)

There are two baths, one male and one female, and they switch them as one is bigger than the other, so do check each time you go!! That afternoon I went down to the bigger one and, having practised in Tokyo diligently, did my double showering and placing my spa towel on the side – even though there was no one else there. Yes, I had this spectacular location all to myself. People often say it's about the journey not the destination, but sometimes you just need to stop and relax and enjoy the destination and think "Yes, life is good, it was so worth coming all the way to Japan for this".

The water is very hot, so there's also a tub of cold water you can drench yourself with using a traditional Japanese pitcher, which I needed several times. Shivering naked in the forest and then diving back into the hot tub is something else.

The next morning I went down to the other onsen, which, although smaller, is just as fabulous, has the same view and once again I had it all to myself.

The changing rooms here have all the amenities you could wish for, and there is also a selection of vinegar drinks and water in the entrance area, so you can heal inside and out.

As much as I love sushi I've gone out of my depth before (raw octopus) and I'm not good on jellified food either (I prefer my tofu fried). I've also heard some kaiseki meals can be a real assault on the stomach. (Now my stomach had not been great on the plane but, ever since eating Japanese it was feeling better and better – I'd even tried the vinegar drinks in the onsen, I was feeling good.)

It's not just that this dinner is so artistic you could display it in the Tate Modern…

It's not just that it is accompanied with descriptive notes that sound like love poems…

It's not just that all of the flavours work together so perfectly…

It's not just the waitress who performs with such drama that just watching her is a pleasant evening's entertainment…

…the absolute perfection is that every single mouthful of this feast is designed to work together.

As much as I love eating, there are times when different foods fight with each other in my tummy.

Every mouthful made my tastebuds, my eyes, my ears, my tongue and my stomach happy.

This is not just food, this is a gastronomic massage of the mind, body and spirit.

We ate:

Appetiser

Smoked salmon and "marriage" of the seasonal vegetables presented in two styles.

Assorted Delicacies:

Crab and kinuta roll

Dried kaki persimmon foie gras

Cream soy milk tofu with shungiku bitter spinach miso

Mustard spinach, boiled soy-flavored shiitake mushroom

Skewered smoked duck and apple

Salmon rice crackers, almonds

Dried yam stems in Tosa style

Eggplant potage, mountain caviar and flying fish roe

Soup

Pumpkin soup, deep fried daikon radish cake, seafood stick, snow peas

(N.B. This is, of course, not the soup but the accompanying sake.)

Sashimi

King Prawn with egg yolk in miso paste

Tuna with daikon radish, lemon and spring onion in vinegar

Grouper with Japanese pepper and daikon radish

Scallop with salted seaweed with Japanese citrus

Ribbon fish with plum

Salted squid with Japanese basil

Deep Fried Tempura

Deep fried icefish dumpling and seasonal vegetable tempura garnished with matcha green tea salt and lemon

Steamed Dish

Steamed Yuba tofu skin and lily root with jade green broth

Main Dish

KAI Hakone's specialty: soy milk meringue hot pot

Rice

Steamed white rice

Miso soup and pickled vegetables

Desserts

Choice of

Cream cheese soufflé drizzled with raspberry sauce, strawberry and mint

Hoji-cha tea crème brûlée

Winter special apple and brioche dessert

Plum wine jelly with fruits

Soy ice cream and sour plum sherbet with seasonal fruits

As much as I loved KAI Hakone, there was a big problem with my room. The management team were so attentive they'd emailed beforehand explaining that there'd be some filming, but they'd be sure to house the camera crew far away from their other hotel guests.

They put them in the suite next to me.

Not only did this mean their coming and going on their late night shoot kept me awake (and I was sooo tired at this point), but also, whenever I opened my balcony windows the cigarette smoke from their balcony blew straight into my room. So much for fresh air.

Even when they quietened down I couldn't sleep. I tried opening the windows for fresh air and to hear the brook louder, I tried closing them, I tried listening to my iPod, nothing worked. In my sleep deprived state I felt like the brook was talking to me. Finally I nodded off for an hour or so.

When I came down to breakfast (after a relaxing soak in the onsen) one look at the grilled fish and I wasn't sure I was going to make it – but after a few bites and a few sips of an excellent cappuccino I was ready to put some Western clothes on and go hunt for Mount Fuji.

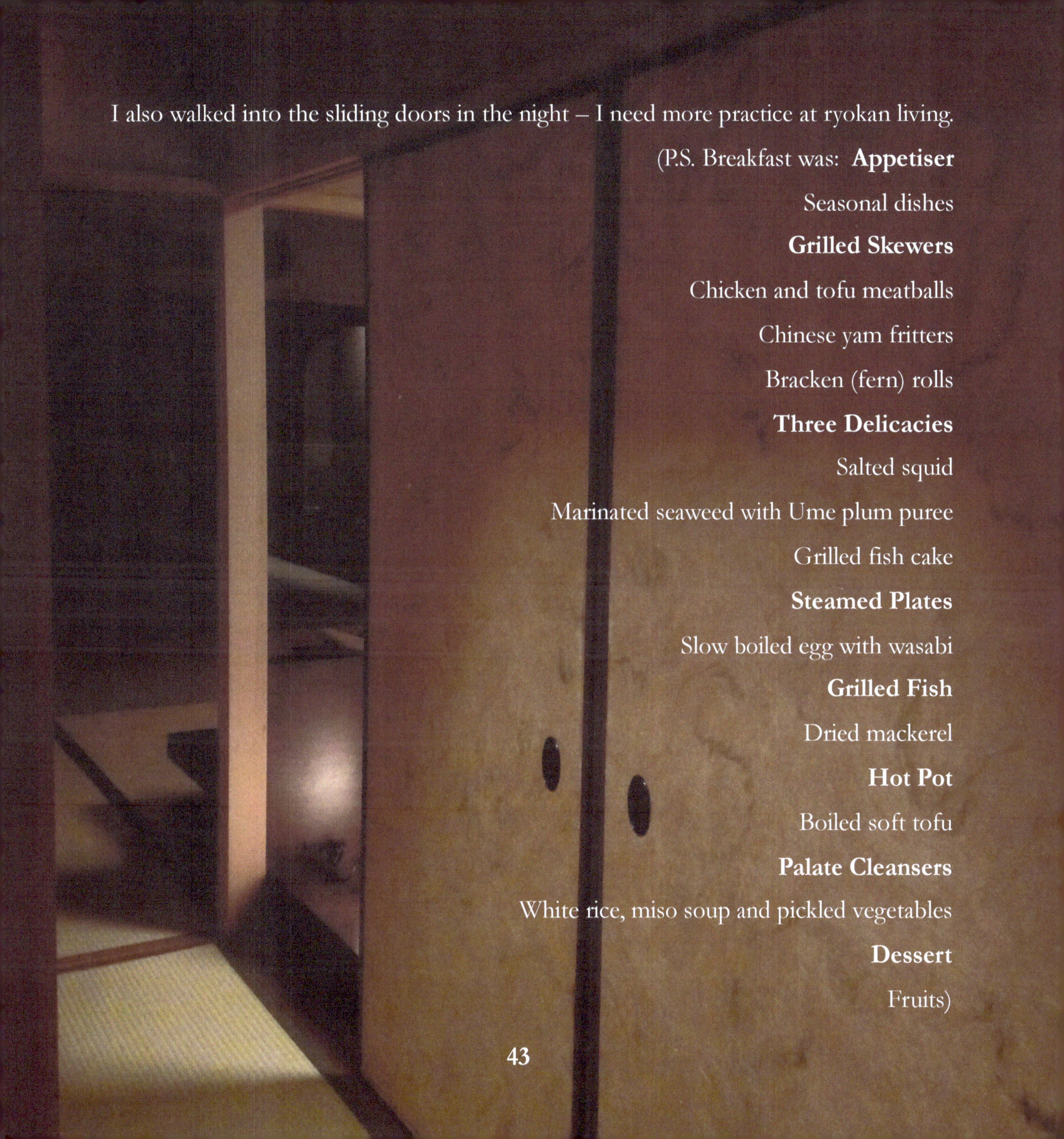

I also walked into the sliding doors in the night – I need more practice at ryokan living.

(P.S. Breakfast was: **Appetiser**

Seasonal dishes

Grilled Skewers

Chicken and tofu meatballs

Chinese yam fritters

Bracken (fern) rolls

Three Delicacies

Salted squid

Marinated seaweed with Ume plum puree

Grilled fish cake

Steamed Plates

Slow boiled egg with wasabi

Grilled Fish

Dried mackerel

Hot Pot

Boiled soft tofu

Palate Cleansers

White rice, miso soup and pickled vegetables

Dessert

Fruits)

250-0312 230 Yumotochaya, Hakonemachi, Ashigara, Shimo-gun Kanagawa, Japan

+81-(0)50-3786-0099

kai-hakone.jp

£265 per room per night Junior Tatami Suite Early Bird Offer including dinner, breakfast and full use of the onsen.

Direct booking on their website.

We took a taxi from Odawara station (and then another to Lake Ashi and back to pick up our luggage and back to the station).

The Sight – Hakone – Mount Fuji from Lake Ashi (and Cable Car)

We took this as a little side trip before heading on to Kyoto as it would have been a crime to be this close to Mount Fuji and not take a peek (or should that be peak). Sorry.

It was a quick taxi to the ferry point, where we booked tickets and had time to walk along the lakefront - which has lovely shops and most importantly a great bakery…

(Japan seems to be like China in that their bakeries are a great place for a little stop or even lunch – we had both). Their chocolate chestnut pastry was stunning (why, oh, why can't we get these in England!)

We had beautiful weather for our lake crossing, clear enough to occasionally glance Mount Fuji and the red torii gates of the local shrine.

Luckily, although we'd been told the cable car was closed, the first section was open – which was just enough for a decent view of Mount Fuji.

The Hotel – Kyoto – Screen

My favourite hotel room in Japan. I picked this one out especially from their website. Screen has a novel concept and also a novel approach to booking; each room is designed and decorated individually (you can read the bios of each designer on their website – some are famous kimono designers, others fashion etc.) so there are pure white rooms, an almost entirely black room, an executive suite that is fabulously red and oriental (kimono designer!) and my room (more on which in a mo)…

If you book through a third party website (Booking.com, Expedia etc.) you may only be able to choose your class of room, rather than the exact room (there are three classes). Reading through the reviews on Tripadvisor I saw everyone had given the hotel five stars… except those who had ended up unwittingly in the black room. (It was not popular. I wish now I'd asked to see it.) In order to avoid ending up in the black room (which is in the same middle class of rooms as my gorgeous room 102) you could book an executive suite, as both executive suites are beautiful. You could also book a generic basic room, however I have had problems in the past when hotels have upgraded me… it's hard to argue with an upgrade, but sometimes it is in effect a downgrade.

To book a specific room you need to go to the hotel's own website, where you can book a class of room at a discount or a specific room at full price, which made my mid class room ever so slightly more expensive than the executive suite. The website is definitely worth viewing as the rooms are effectively an art exhibition, but it is a little tricky to book through. It's easy to add a breakfast, but at around £15 you could get a cheaper breakfast locally – especially if you want to head out early.

Room 102 has a fluffy pink carpet, its own hallway that opens out on to a spacious room. The bed is a low, comfortable futon style, facing a black lacquered consol with TV, gadgets…

…(most importantly for me an exceptional sound system that I could plug my iPod into) and drawers with coffee maker. There is a stunning raised tatami platform with traditional Japanese table and cushions (in the "lucky" black and gold pattern I fell in love with on their website) where there's a black lacquer gift box of goodies. The room also has floor to ceiling windows overlooking a small courtyard with a water feature. And then there was the bathroom… By now I expected the top of the range loo, was impressed by the second black lacquer box with goodies, plus robe and towel (probably more slippers just for the bathroom… I was getting blind to slippers by now, they were everywhere) but this bathroom goes one better than the rest… it has a hot tub. Yes, just perfect for tired travellers coming down with a cold.

(Please remember if you see a tatami mat you must NOT walk on it in shoes or toilet slippers.)

Although the journey from Hakone had gone fairly smoothly and we'd seen a beautiful sunset from the train, I was feeling low with a combination of lack of sleep and cold coming on and was divided about whether to leave the hotel once we'd arrived. Luckily we were in time for room service (see Restaurant - Kyoto) and I got to eat at my Japanese table and… when asked if they could organise a massage they were slightly surprised I'd questioned it. As in many countries massage is such a part of the culture here they don't put it on the guest information. So I was able to retire to my room and enjoy a hot tub, in room dining and a fabulous Shiatsu massage (see The Massage – Kyoto) which gave me the best chance of getting a good night's sleep and set me up for a very long day of sightseeing. (Although I still wasn't sleeping properly and if you'd told me then it'd be another few weeks before I got back to normal I couldn't have handled it!)

The hotel staff are fantastically polite and helpful (without them we would never have known about the night time temple opening). As well as our rooms and excellent breakfast in the restaurant there was a small lobby area and café seating, but I will say that I did feel slightly out of place in the restaurant and when we asked about eating there we were told it was closed.

The hotel was exactly what I needed but looking back at the hotel's website I'm surprised we weren't shown around other common areas of the hotel (there may be a rooftop bar) as it looks like there should have been more (it could have just been me being ridiculously sleep deprived). Also when we arrived back later on our second day we were too late for room service and the receptionist couldn't help us with any advice about where to eat locally. There were several good eating options around the corner which we found but personally I wouldn't recommend them because of the smoking.

640-1 Shimogoryomae-cho, Teramachi Marutamachi-sagaru, Nakagyo-ku, Kyoto 604-0995

+81 75-252-1113

Access by train: 10 minute walk east of Marutamachi Station (Karasuma subway line), 7 minute walk west of Keihan Marutamachi Station (Keihan main line)

Access by taxi: 15 minute taxi ride from Kyoto Station

Room 102 (specifically booked) £216 per night including breakfast (one person)

Executive Suite £210 per night including breakfast (one person)

Booked directly via the hotel's website.

As at December 2015

The Massage – Kyoto – Room Service at Screen

I was delighted to be able to have an in room massage, and the great thing (aside from being able to go to sleep afterwards) was being able to pre-game by having a long bubble session in the hot tub in my bathroom. The hotel supplies pyjamas (it seems customary for Japanese hotels - some even provide both Western and traditional yukatas).

My therapist knocked so gently I didn't hear her, it took a call from reception to open the door. She seemed a little nervous, perhaps because we didn't speak the same language. I must admit it was one of the trickiest communication experiences I've had, and I've had a lot of massages from people who I don't share a language with.

Unlike the Shiatsu massage in London, which I had on the floor on towels, this one was on my bed, but as it was such a low, big bed it was pretty much the same thing.

Technically it was excellent (as far as I could tell from the one other Shiatsu massage I've had) and she really helped me to ease out muscles which were tense from travelling. (Mind you, I'd been in the onsen at KAI Hakone that morning and the night before… not to mention the onsen and hot tub in Tokyo). I think I even dozed off at one point and snored a little.

The only challenges were her telling me when to turn over and turn on my side (I do love a side lying massage) and at one point my tired brain thought she was telling me to turn around, as in put my head at the bottom of the bed. Then she quietly assured me she was finished, left and I went straight to sleep. (The nice thing about no tipping is that I never had to think what to tip her.)

6,480 yen for one hour massage, approximately £35

As at December 201

The Sight – Kyoto - Fushimi Inari Shrine

I want to say "Kyoto is lousy with temples", which could be misunderstood, but I mean you are spoiled for choice here. Unlike Tokyo where I found it hard to choose because there were only a few places far apart I found appealing, in Kyoto it felt like every corner had another famous temple.

As the Fushimi Inari Shrine is commonly featured on the front of most Japanese guidebooks and is proudly proclaimed as the number one sight in Kyoto on Tripadvisor I figured this might be worth a look.

I really loved it.

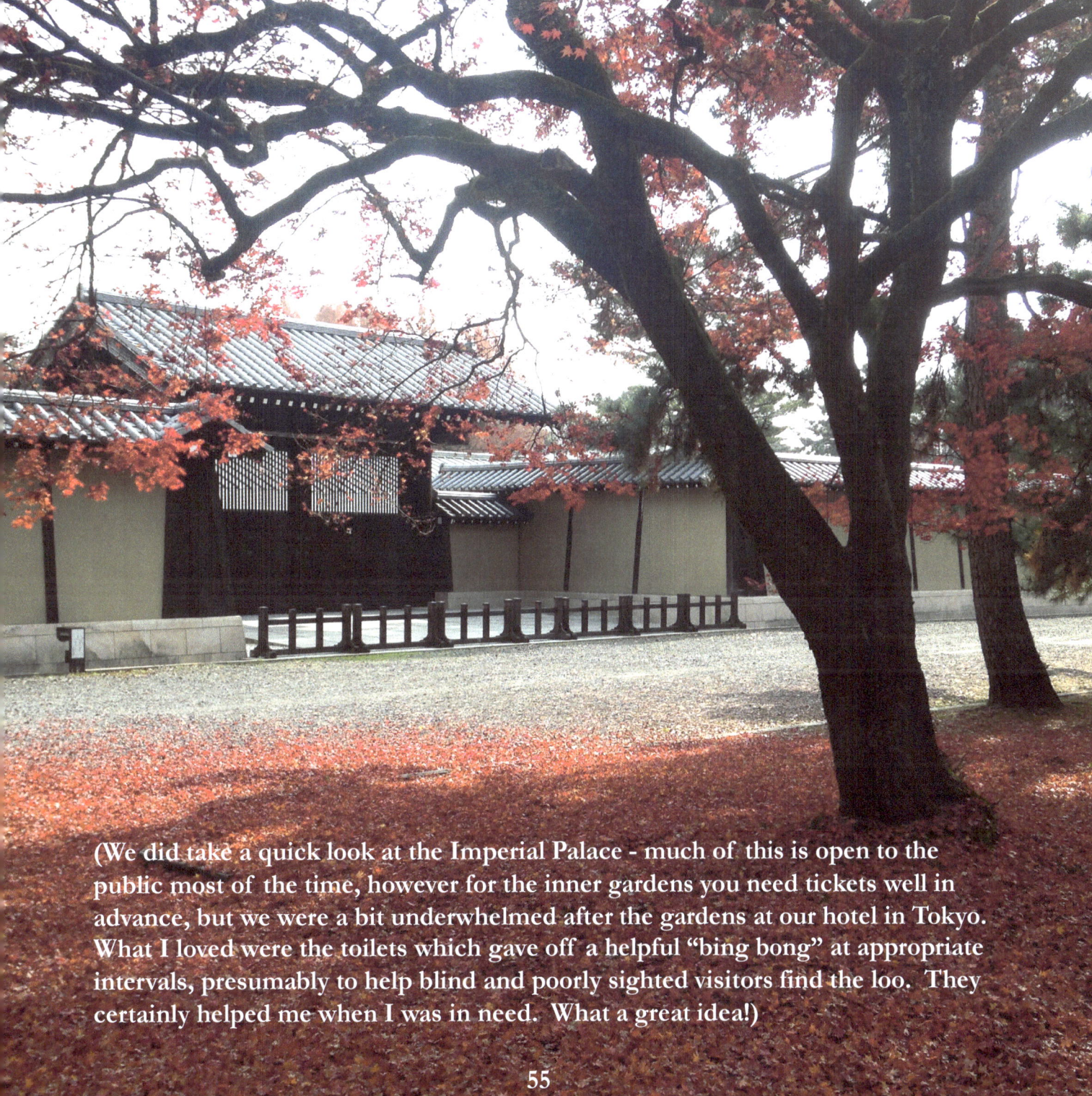

(We did take a quick look at the Imperial Palace - much of this is open to the public most of the time, however for the inner gardens you need tickets well in advance, but we were a bit underwhelmed after the gardens at our hotel in Tokyo. What I loved were the toilets which gave off a helpful "bing bong" at appropriate intervals, presumably to help blind and poorly sighted visitors find the loo. They certainly helped me when I was in need. What a great idea!)

As you leave the train station and walk up to the shrine there are myriads of stalls and shops (you can get great food for a pittance here) and it is noisy and busy. Don't be surprised if you're asked to take photos of Japanese people dressed up as geisha, it's a popular place for everyone to be a tourist, but as you start up the walk of the red torii gates the noise and bustle falls away.

There are also bamboo forests on the way up - I actually followed a little Japanese man up a side path into the forest (and then realized he was probably just walking home, not sightseeing).

The red gates are not actually the shrine (or should I say shrines), they are only advertising local businesses and are donated and maintained by those businesses (it's a lot of red paint needed to keep them fresh). The fact they are a "commercial signpost" doesn't stop them becoming more and more magical as you head away from the crowds and up Mount Inari (yes, Inari sushi is named after the mountain) – especially if you don't understand the symbols.

Nearer the summit there are views of the whole of Kyoto, many, many small shrines, a little shop where you can enjoy excellent espresso (and boiled eggs if you are so inclined) and…

...as I walked around the top and back around to the sushi restaurant I saw the red leaves of the Japanese oak falling softly on top of the torii gates.

I was often alone at this point, as the crowds had thinned out, and this, for me, is Fushimi Inari Shrine.

Free

December 2015

The Massage – Kyoto – Anma at Asahido Massage Therapy Clinic

They were very surprised to see white people at the door. (I quite like this - it means I've done my homework and found the local hangout.) I'd found it hard to find much being offered besides Shiatsu on the traditional side, so was very excited about Anma:

"Anma means to press (an) and rub (ma). It also means to spread peace by rubbing or to calm with the hands. Anma is one of the oldest forms of massage in the world (from ancient China over 7,000 years ago), and it is the oldest form of bodywork in the Orient. The anma technique was brought to Japan and was further refined and developed into its own therapeutic art form."

Like Shiatsu it is performed without oil and clothed (pyjamas are lent free of charge).

It took us a while to find Asahido, although it's in a grid like area so should have been easier (blame my sleep deprived brain). The website does not do it justice. I find that the Japanese are so enamoured of cleanliness that they often use "clean" as a selling point, whereas I read that as so basic it doesn't really advertise the place well.

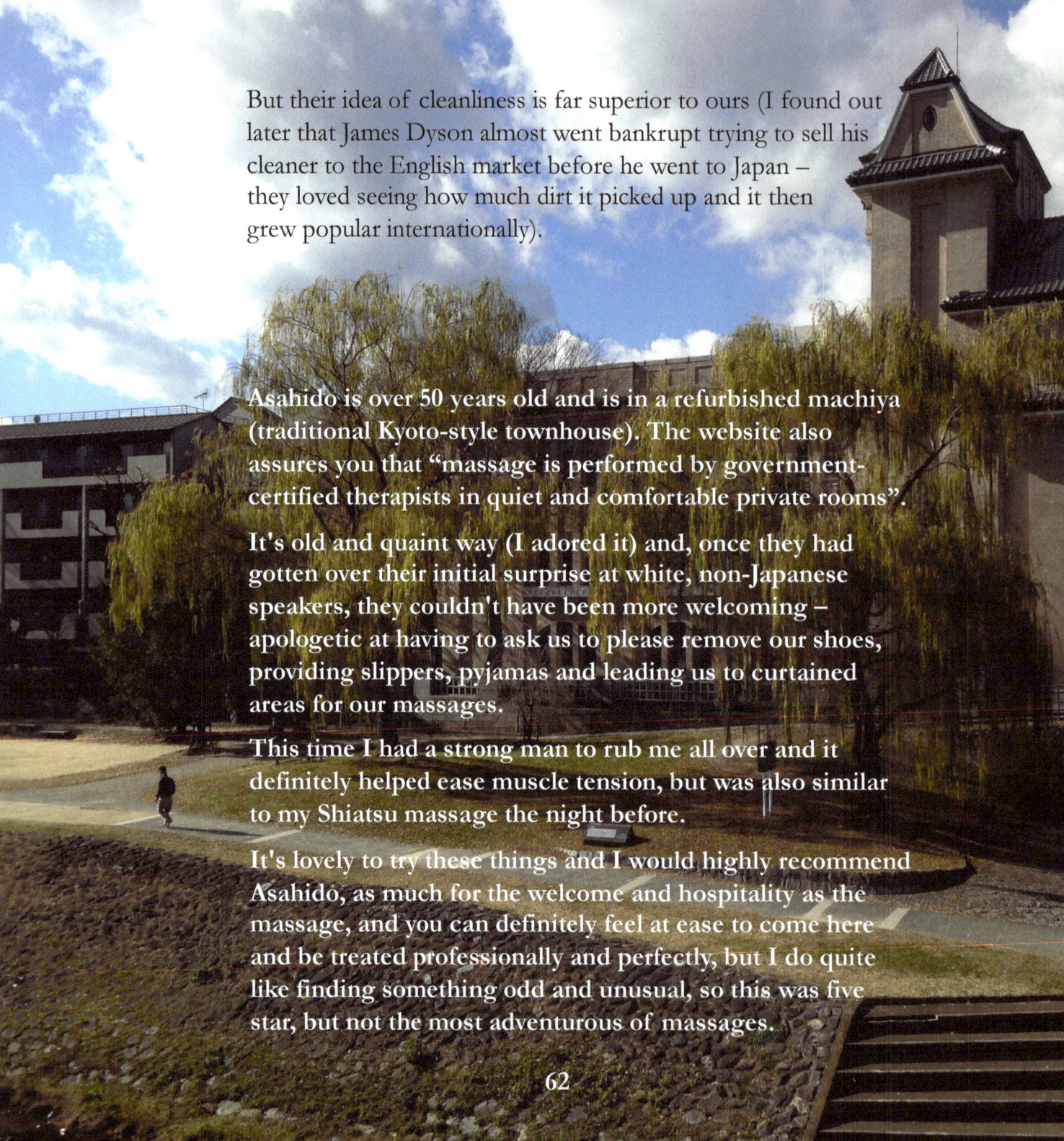

But their idea of cleanliness is far superior to ours (I found out later that James Dyson almost went bankrupt trying to sell his cleaner to the English market before he went to Japan – they loved seeing how much dirt it picked up and it then grew popular internationally).

Asahido is over 50 years old and is in a refurbished machiya (traditional Kyoto-style townhouse). The website also assures you that "massage is performed by government-certified therapists in quiet and comfortable private rooms".

It's old and quaint way (I adored it) and, once they had gotten over their initial surprise at white, non-Japanese speakers, they couldn't have been more welcoming – apologetic at having to ask us to please remove our shoes, providing slippers, pyjamas and leading us to curtained areas for our massages.

This time I had a strong man to rub me all over and it definitely helped ease muscle tension, but was also similar to my Shiatsu massage the night before.

It's lovely to try these things and I would highly recommend Asahido, as much for the welcome and hospitality as the massage, and you can definitely feel at ease to come here and be treated professionally and perfectly, but I do quite like finding something odd and unusual, so this was five star, but not the most adventurous of massages.

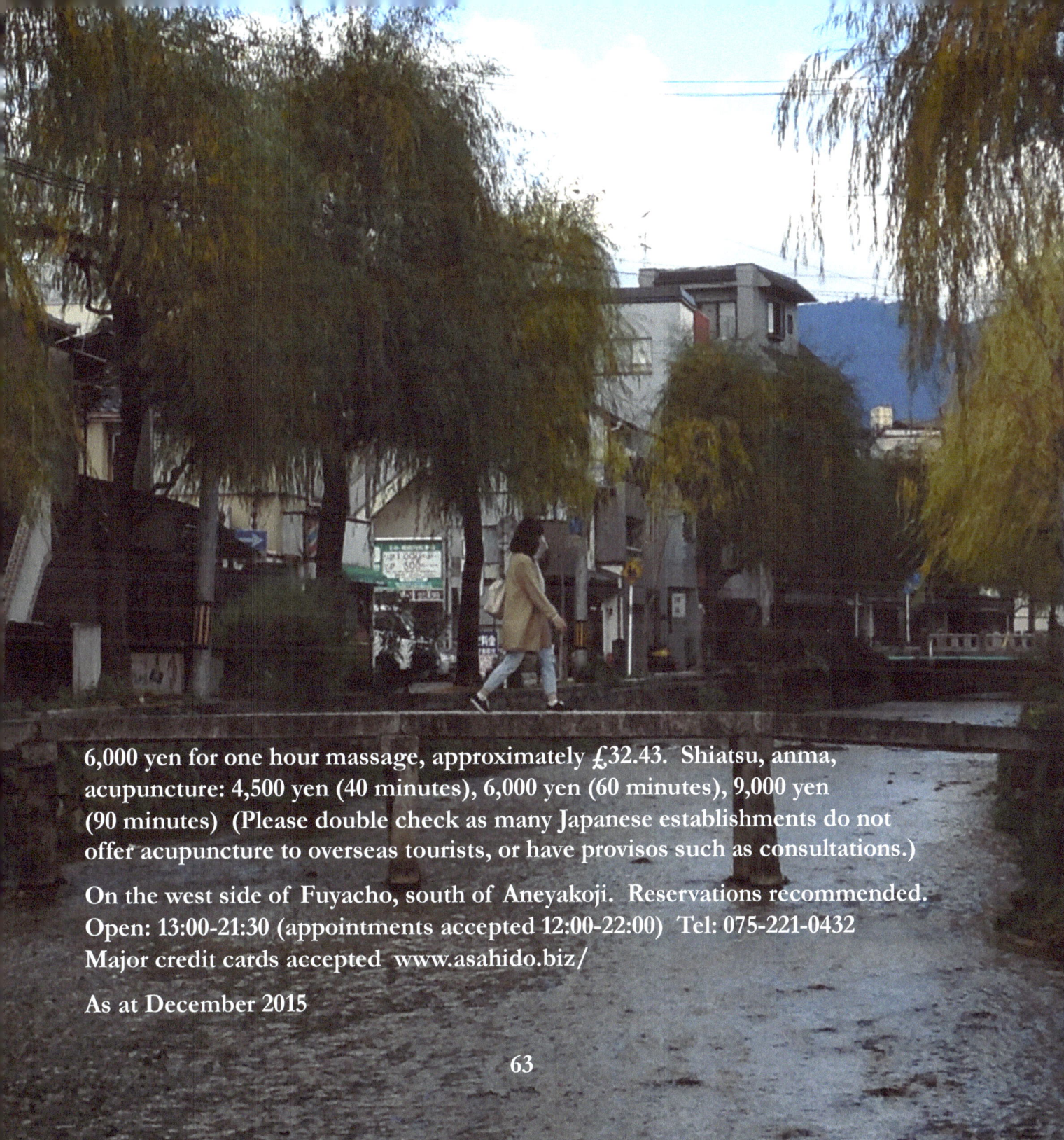

6,000 yen for one hour massage, approximately £32.43. Shiatsu, anma, acupuncture: 4,500 yen (40 minutes), 6,000 yen (60 minutes), 9,000 yen (90 minutes) (Please double check as many Japanese establishments do not offer acupuncture to overseas tourists, or have provisos such as consultations.)

On the west side of Fuyacho, south of Aneyakoji. Reservations recommended. Open: 13:00-21:30 (appointments accepted 12:00-22:00) Tel: 075-221-0432 Major credit cards accepted www.asahido.biz/

As at December 2015

The Sight – Kyoto - Night Time at Tenryuji Temple

The lady at Asahido was very apologetic when we told her where we were going. "No, this temple will not be open."

But in this case the local knowledge from Screen (our hotel) trumped her local knowledge because the temple was having a special night time festival.

Normally, as with many other temples, closing time is dusk, so we were extremely lucky in our timing and in our choice of hotel to be able to catch this.

Tenruiji Temple is vast - it encompasses gardens and bamboo forests, a famous tea house, and walkways, all lit up for the night with lanterns.

This being Japan, as well as beautiful natural scenery and lighting we were also "blessed" with a popular cartoon character messing about taking photos with people in the middle of the bamboo. I have no idea, really, no idea, but it was moments like this that gave me an insight into the Japanese character (if there is such a thing); serious, polite, deferential, strictly following the rules (you should see a Japanese airport queue – they can queue politely in up to five lanes – without barriers!) and then giggly, silly, over the moon, childlike excitement about a full size cartoon character. Just a joy to be around.

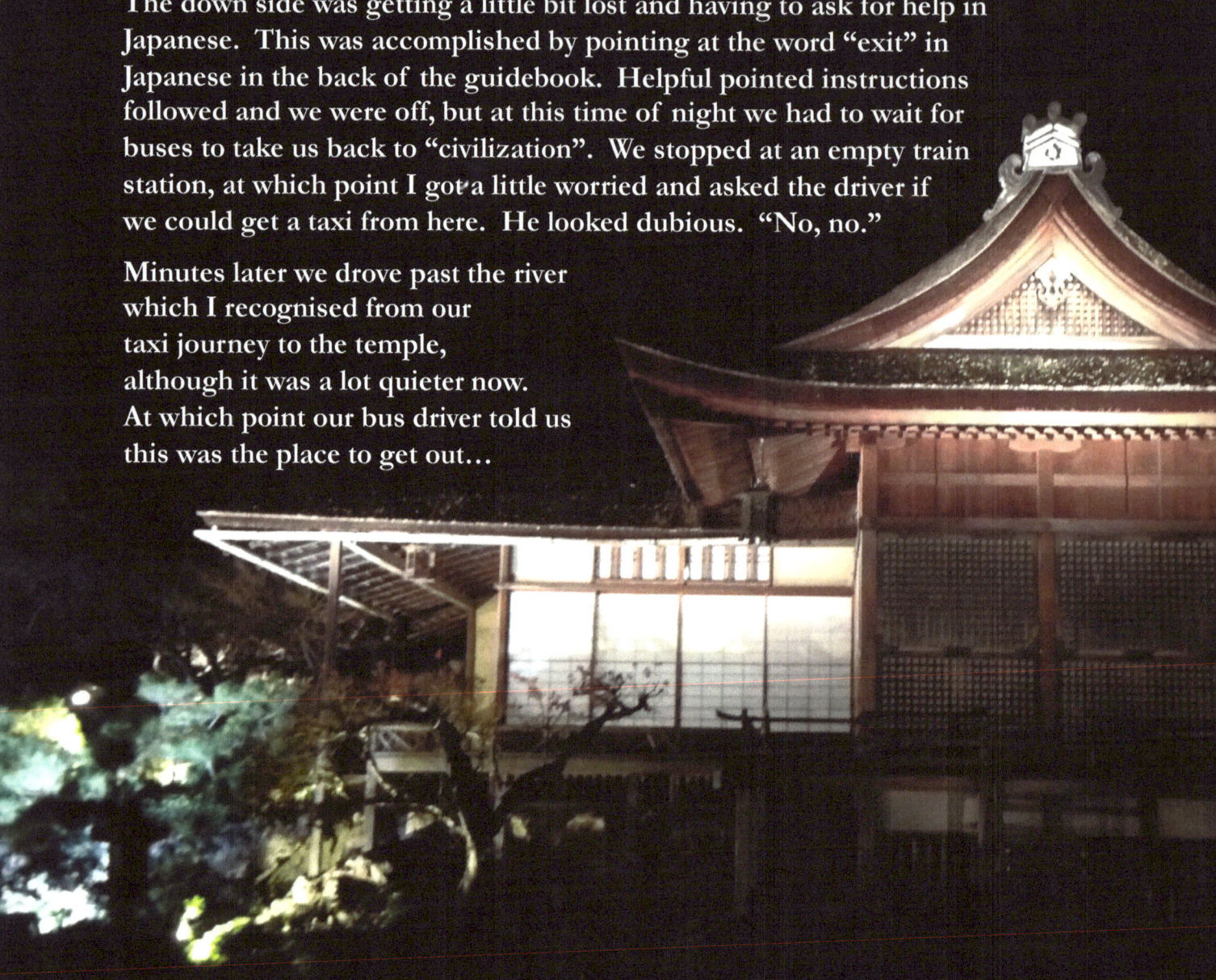

The down side was getting a little bit lost and having to ask for help in Japanese. This was accomplished by pointing at the word "exit" in Japanese in the back of the guidebook. Helpful pointed instructions followed and we were off, but at this time of night we had to wait for buses to take us back to "civilization". We stopped at an empty train station, at which point I got a little worried and asked the driver if we could get a taxi from here. He looked dubious. "No, no."

Minutes later we drove past the river which I recognised from our taxi journey to the temple, although it was a lot quieter now. At which point our bus driver told us this was the place to get out…

…AND THEN HE STOPPED THE BUS. Yes, even with other passengers onboard (who didn't seem to mind,) he got off the bus and stood with us until he had managed to hail us a taxi. Then waved goodbye and went back to his bus.

I was open mouthed. Such customer service is rare, especially when there is no tipping and especially when the whole evening and the bus itself, was free.

Tenryuji Temple - http://www.tenryuji.com/en/

Free, but normally 500-800 yen depending on the ticket - £3 to £5

As at December 2015

The Restaurant – Kyoto – Room Service at Screen and a Few More Food and Drink Tips

Room service at Screen was just a light plate of sushi before bed, but I adored this, the look, the flavours. I was being truly spoiled in Japan.

Aside from being waited on hand and foot in our hotel, we also ate a lot of great sushi and hot food from street vendors on our way back from Fushimi Inari. But what I really wanted to be able to recommend was Inari sushi eaten on Mount Inari – so I was devastated when I got back down to find it was all gone.

I can however highly recommend the espresso near the summit. They also sell boiled eggs.

Oh and Pavilion Court is also a lovely stop – they do delicious pancakes with chestnuts, opposite the Shoren-in Temple.

2,480 yen approximately £13.40 for sushi at Screen

As at December 2015

Train from Kyoto to Wakayama

Okay, this was when I realized how spoilt we had become with the shinkansen. I don't think we did it right. I spent a long time talking to the lady in Tourist Information, but somewhere between her nervous description and actually doing it something may have got lost in translation.

It didn't help that my taxi driver had somehow thought I was just showing him the hotel's card by way of conversation instead of my first stop to pick up my client and our luggage… and had headed straight for the station. I was watching our progress on Google Maps so realized and turned him round, but it was a delay.

We were now heading into rush hour, using the local stopping trains - this was about to be a more interesting journey.

Everything I'd learned about the Japanese, the politeness and helpfulness was now all about to be crushed.

Do not get in the way of a Japanese commuter.

We were coming down escalators onto a platform as trains stopped and doors opened. I felt a wave of panic as a sea of commuters headed for us (I do not exaggerate).

We were fairly lucky in the trains we actually boarded - many of them were practically empty as we were travelling away from Kyoto, including one with a pink carriage especially for girls, and we were able to sit for most of the way, which was lucky as the entire journey took us well over three hours.

Once we were out of the commuter crush, and on our way to Wakayama I was quickly reminded again of how helpful the Japanese people tend to be. Our train divided, so our half went on to Wakayama and the other half went to Osaka Airport. Because we had cases with us, we were asked about ten times by different passengers if we knew that we were not in fact going to the airport on this train.

We messed up, because we took the cheap route, but I believe the fastest route would be to take the shinkansen to Shin Osaka which would have taken around 14 minutes (around £15) and then local train about 1 hour from Osaka to Wakayama for a few quid.

The Hotel – Granvia Wakayama

I always think I get exactly what I need from my hotel (even if it's not what I want!) I'd booked a Double and Superior Double online, after my email to book Japanese style rooms (which I'd seen on their website) didn't get a reply. Once there I asked for a Japanese room and was told none were available – however when I went to my room the wind was whipping round the corner - there was no way I'd be able to sleep in there. So they gave me a Japanese style room for one night. Which was when I realised that all of my jumping up and down about trying a Japanese style room was ill-advised… I couldn't understand the instructions and couldn't work the kettle. As for sleeping on a futon or having a raised tatami area, I'd already been so spoilt in Hakone and Kyoto, and even Tokyo, that any hotel would have to be pretty special at this point to impress me.

The hotel did have good rooms, the lobby has a heaven sent choice of pillows, and the chance to try a Japanese style room… It's a very good hotel, but the Double Room is so small that I finally understood what so many guidebooks say about Japanese hotel rooms. (In fact, as I was now developing quite the respiratory infection this room was great because I ran a long shower and the whole room got steamy.)

The breakfast buffet was excellent including Japanese specialties and a grill to put fish on (I stuck with the pastries) and was much needed for our walk.

The location of the hotel was perfect as a base for our day trip although, next time, I would stay at least a day on the coast (some beautiful hotels down there), but this also gave us a good base for the return flight and, if the weather had been awful and we had to skip the Kumano Kodo, it was close enough for us to go shopping in Osaka. (Granvia Wakayama is connected to the Wakayama train station.)

My biggest complaint about the hotel was it just felt like a shopping centre. Although I'm sure the vending machines (which sell things like hot fish and chips!) are fantastic for people travelling, I was looking forward to a more atmospheric hotel. When we went to the restaurant floor it really did feel like we were in a mall.

We ate at the Chinese restaurant on both nights, which was wonderful, and we just stocked up on snacks at the train station shops (which are pretty awesome by the way) before we headed to the Kumano Kodo.

Our reception staff were wonderful about information, booking our taxi to Nachi Falls even though it did take three phone calls (the concierge was very concerned that it was far too expensive for us and didn't want to book it because the train would be so much cheaper) and a long chat with the taxi driver at reception (and even then he didn't seem to always understand what we were doing – there were a few worried moments when we thought he might abandon us in the middle of the mountains).

Although we booked three nights here, when we returned from our walk and I asked them if we could cancel our last night they were more than helpful, understanding that perhaps for the last day and night of our "once in a lifetime" trip to Japan, Osaka might be a little bit more exciting than Wakayama.

Tomodacho 5-18, Wakayama, 640-8342 Tel: 817-342-53-333

Superior Double Room - Non Smoking - £82 per night including breakfast (Standard £68 per night)

The Sight – Nachi Falls and the Daimon-zaka on the Kumano Kodo

We left early in the morning, getting into our taxi just as it was light but the sun had not yet risen. The first part of the journey was dull; office blocks and motorways, broken only by the

sight of the big yellow ball, the sun rising so determinedly that it resounded "The Land of the Rising Sun".

Then we turned off into the mountains. This was the reason we chose to make the journey by car, so we could see all of this. Ridges of mountains, silhouettes shadowing each other, giants in shades of grey.

Or at least this was why I thought we had taken the car, but there was so much more to see. The autumn colours ("koyo" or "momiji") were so glorious that they made a mockery of the famous Japanese white blossoms (why settle for one colour when you can have a whole autumnal palette?) The mountains would have been reason alone for this journey, the autumn colours reason alone, but there was something else, the waters. I believe this is the river that meets up with Nachi Falls, but never, in all my travels, have I seen waters of this colour. Perhaps it was the sky reflecting, perhaps the minerals in the riverbed, but there was something magical about the colour of this river.

The Kumano Kodo is a sacred pilgrimage, a walk in and around the Kii mountains. It is one of only two pilgrimages listed as UNESCO heritage sites and is twinned with the other; the St James Way or Camino de Santiago in Portugal/Spain (although you can start the Camino anywhere). (Strangely enough, when I went on retreat in Sedona, Arizona in April 2016 I chose, unusually for me, to share my room with another person. Along with many other coincidences, when I mentioned I had been to Japan she asked if I had ever heard of the Kumano Kodo - she was planning to walk it the next year).

Many people walk the whole route, staying at small ryokans along the way and this is definitely something I am thinking of doing in the future (not least to try out the tiny onsens also along the route) but this was December, this was an eight day trip and I was accompanying a lady in her 60s for whom just this section of the walk was a challenge.

I had read conflicting information about the walk and although Japanese maps are a lot more efficient and less artistic than Chinese maps (don't get me started on getting lost on mountains in China) I was still confused about how long, how steep and how remote our walk was going to be (and also whether we would be able to get a taxi back down). This was another reason for starting early.

One of the very important life lessons I learned on the top of Huangshan in China (I learnt so much in that one day!) was to respect the point of no return. This is mainly taken from ships – there is a point in the crossing when a ship used to sound its horn to indicate that this was the point of no return – it was necessary at this point to go forwards to the new shore rather than to return to the old one – very important if you were a stowaway, as after the horn they wouldn't turn back to put you off the ship (there's no telling if they would throw you overboard though).

Anyway what I learned on Huangshan is this, pack enough water, food and have enough energy to go back the way you came and, when you reach the point where you feel you can just about retrace your steps but no more, then take stock. If you do not absolutely know your way forward or are 100% confident you can reach the destination then turn right round and go back the way you came. There is no shame in this. Many explorers have had to do it, but best to do it whilst you still have the supplies and energy to get back. So my plan was this; set off from the base of the walk early, so that if necessary we would have time to walk back to the base. I also had details of a number of hotels nearby in case we could not get buses or trains back to Wakayama. (I do learn from my mistakes, well some of them.)

So, I had some information from Psychologies magazine, some from the website which listed the walk from the base to Nachi Falls as three and a half hours, and other conflicting sources. We had water, we had snacks, the lady I was accompanying had walking poles (okay, I'll admit it I just had a mini rucksack and carrier bags with the snacks – I wasn't a real hiker) and we were ready for an adventure.

In the end the walk we took was intoxicatingly beautiful, fairly easy physically, the signs were only a little bit confusing and there was not only a bank of taxis on the summit, but also a Post Office, souvenir shops, a small town, a place to rent costumes and stacks of elderly Japanese people flying up and down the steps, but before we knew that it all felt a bit daunting.

Let me try to clarify.

From the official base (where the buses stop) on the main road (which has lovely toilets and vending machines selling hot and cold cans of drink), you cross the road and follow the signs. It's a lot like following Public Footpath signs in England, although it did feel initially as if we were walking up someone's driveway. These people also have extra vending machines in their gardens.

Once we reached a small ornate bridge and a shop renting costumes I was more confident we were on the right path.

A little further and I could see the Daimon-zaka, a pathway with ancient stone steps circling upwards through the trees. I felt "Yes, this is the right place, the place my heart was leading me."

We walked alone, in silence, as a pilgrimage. Because of the moss on the steps and a little morning dampness I took it slowly. This also gave me time to reflect on and absorb the beauty of the trees. Two of them, a sign told me, were 800 years old and were considered a "husband and wife". I decided to give one a hug. I was struggling, still not sleeping, and the question on my mind was "How can I do this? Make it through this trip?"

As I hugged the tree I felt the answer deep within me; "Your strength comes from nature. All you have to do is touch nature, hug a tree and the strength will come to you." (Hugging trees has now become an important daily practice for me as I make massive changes in my life.)

My main complaint about the Daimon-zaka is that it's just too short. Before long I emerged into a clearing with a bench and a signpost up to the next part of the walk (it's on the right – there's a concrete car park building directly in front).

Turning right I found myself in the little town. You follow the path a little to the right and then left up another steep set of steps. But should you go wrong, you're in a town of helpful Japanese people – I wouldn't worry. The Post Office is on the right and you can buy beautiful gift cards here.

There was no rush as I was still waiting for my client to catch up. I had time to wander through the souvenir shops. There's a tea garden (no actual tea at this time of year), bonsai and stunning views of the hills dropping down to the ocean, and, of course, shrines, the pagoda and the waterfall. I could hear it before I could see it and I took my time, enjoying the gardens, trying to fight the desire to rush.

I took a left across a gorgeous red bridge, which leads around to the red shrines.

Although people take so many pictures of the shrines and the pagoda these are actually nothing of spiritual significance – they're only here to mark the spot of the real shrines; the waterfall and the trees.

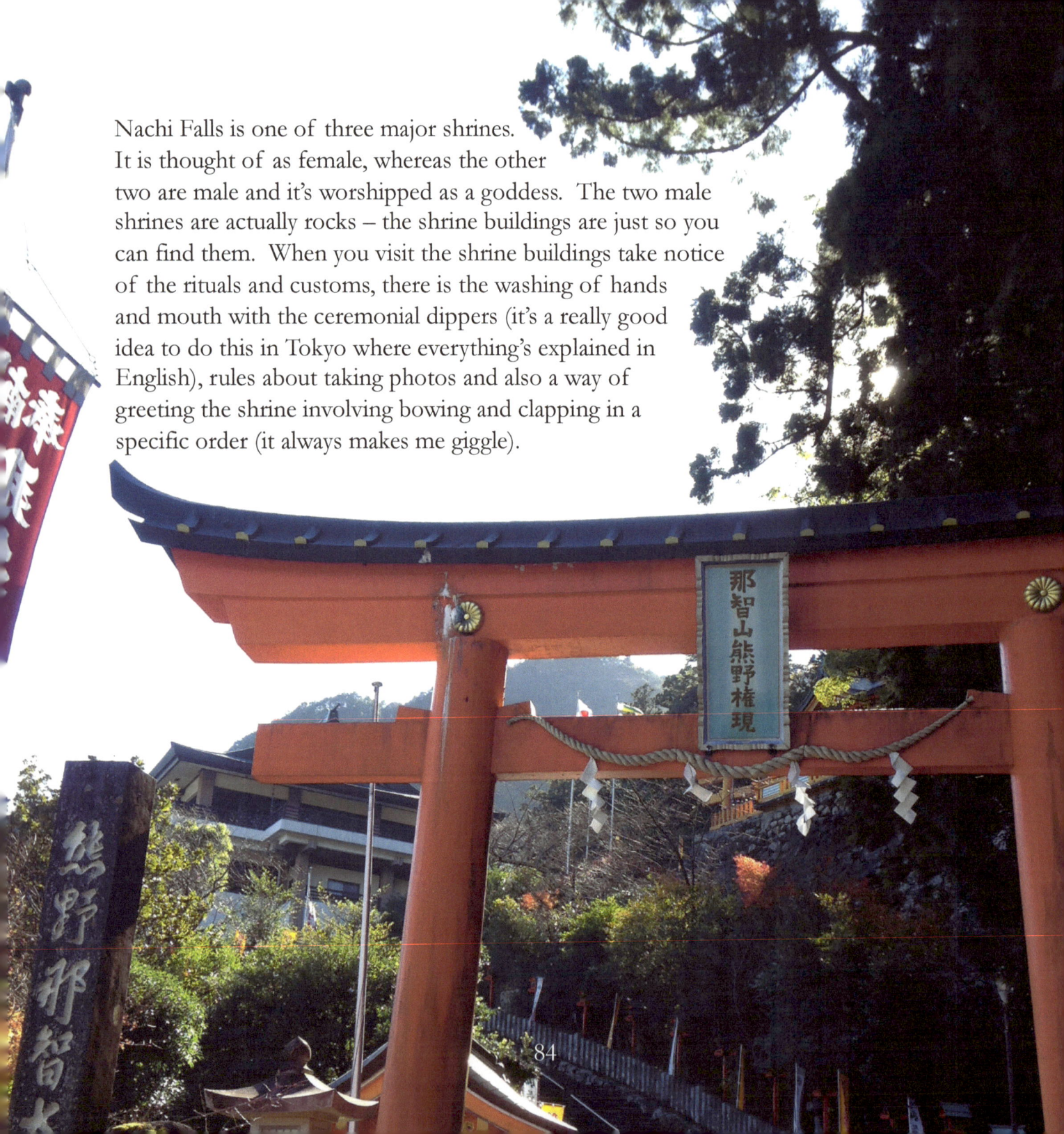

Nachi Falls is one of three major shrines. It is thought of as female, whereas the other two are male and it's worshipped as a goddess. The two male shrines are actually rocks – the shrine buildings are just so you can find them. When you visit the shrine buildings take notice of the rituals and customs, there is the washing of hands and mouth with the ceremonial dippers (it's a really good idea to do this in Tokyo where everything's explained in English), rules about taking photos and also a way of greeting the shrine involving bowing and clapping in a specific order (it always makes me giggle).

Although I wasn't feeling the shrine buildings, something drew me to a gnarled, ancient tree, which seemed to hover in midair behind one of them. In fact, as I came around to the front of it I saw that the ground dipped down to the roots. The body of the tree and the roots looked almost as if they had been carved out; this is an ancient shrine which you approach with the same ritual as the shrine buildings. There was something very special and beautiful about this tree.

I couldn't help thinking of "The Lord of the Rings" and Elvish kingdoms.

And then on to the pagoda and the falls themselves (or herself). You pay a few yen to go inside and climb the pagoda, which is nice enough, but I enjoyed the view from beneath the pagoda best.

As I pondered the falls I felt questions I'd been carrying fall into place. I had three relationships that were filling my head (keeping me awake) and in Hakone, as the brook whispered to me through the night, the one thing that made sense was "one disastrous relationship at a time".

Under the falls I was thinking of my romantic relationship, my beloved and ideas that I had been reflecting on throughout the trip. I had never believed in the idea of "the love of your life" (although I hadn't believed in "the One" until I met him either, and he was not "the love of my life". When "the One" came tumbling into my life I knew I wouldn't have long with him but he knocked my life completely off course…

…a lonely course where I wasn't letting anyone in, where I was afraid to love and be loved, to be hurt, and he made me believe that I deserved better and that I could open up and enjoy love again).

Under the falls I had to admit that my beloved was the love of my life, even if I never saw him again, spoke to him. I had to admit that in my heart that was the truth. (And then I had to go and tell him, which was so much harder.)

Unfortunately because we walked back the same way we missed the entrance to the path that takes you up close to the falls, but the Daimon-zaka is definitely worth a second walk.

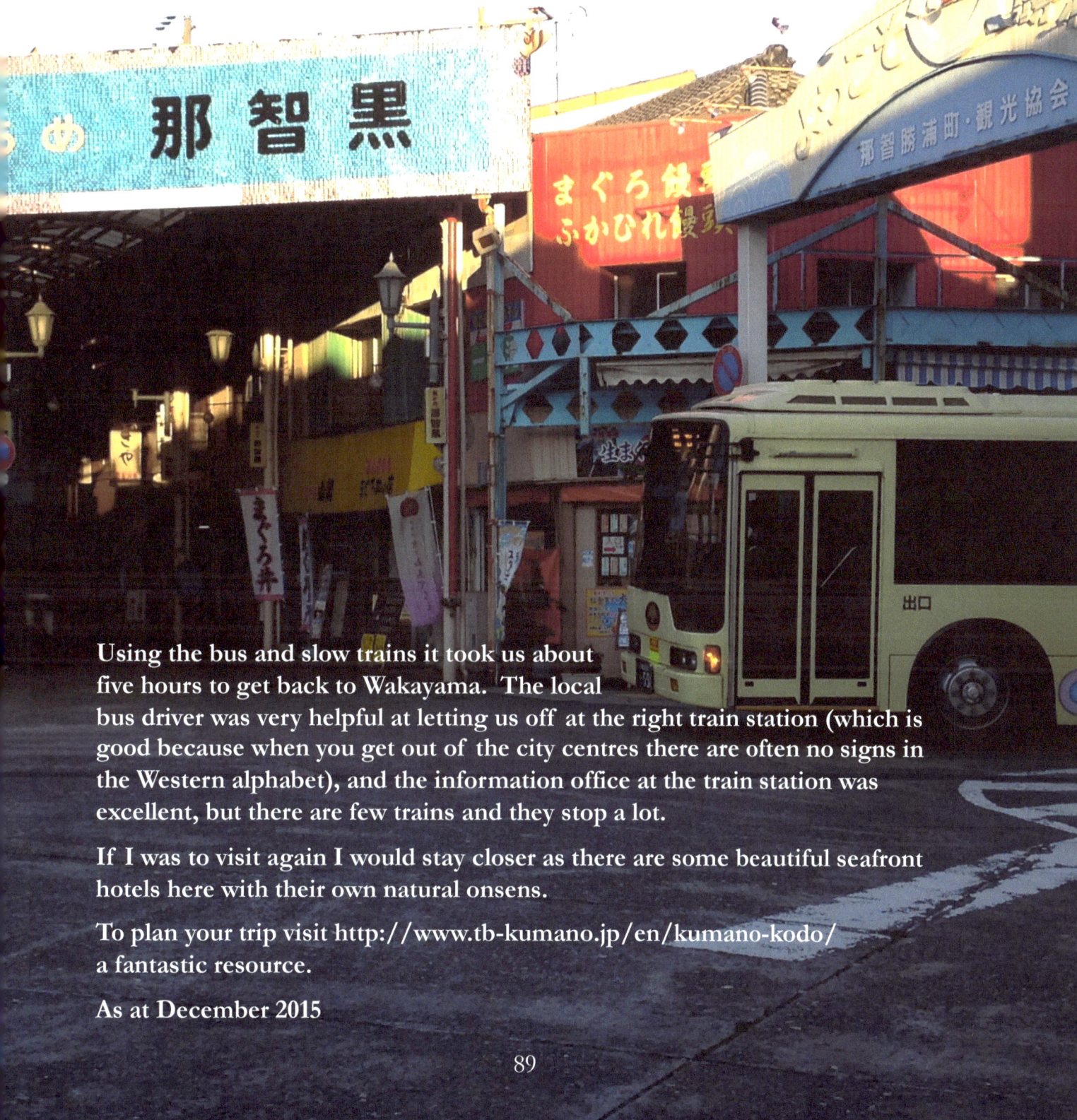

Using the bus and slow trains it took us about five hours to get back to Wakayama. The local bus driver was very helpful at letting us off at the right train station (which is good because when you get out of the city centres there are often no signs in the Western alphabet), and the information office at the train station was excellent, but there are few trains and they stop a lot.

If I was to visit again I would stay closer as there are some beautiful seafront hotels here with their own natural onsens.

To plan your trip visit http://www.tb-kumano.jp/en/kumano-kodo/ a fantastic resource.

As at December 2015

Train from Wakayama to Osaka

About an hour. Very cheap (especially compared to the shinkansen).

The Sight – Osaka Castle and The Santa Orchestra

Although I ventured out to look at the castle up close, I'd have to say the best views of it were still from my room, or from the rooftop bar.

I add also the sight that wowed me as I came down the escalators in one of the shopping complexes near the New Otani – a whole orchestra dressed as Santas!

Japan takes Christmas to heart and I just love how much they adore Father Christmas. (Although I'd better add another sight as it's pretty seasonal and you might not be as lucky as me!)

Osaka - Hotel New Otani (or New Hotel Otani)

Although Nachi Falls was, for me, the highlight of our trip to Japan, the five hour journey back and the bug I'd picked up (not to mention the insomnia) was taking its toll on me, so I really wasn't up to looking for the hidden joys of Wakayama.

Instead I went to one of my failsafe back-up plans – book into an amazing hotel. Luckily Osaka has some of the most incredible hotels in the world (in fact, if you're keen to stay in a particular world class hotel chain you could do a lot worse than look in Osaka). (This is also great if you're booking online at the last minute as I've had discounts before of 80%.) I didn't get quite that discount on this hotel, but two Castle View rooms were just in budget (with the cancellation and refund of our last night in the Granvia Wakayama) and I figured that even if we didn't have the energy to leave the hotel we'd be okay with the insane number of facilities inside (including, most importantly for me, another onsen and a spa). Also extremely importantly, the New Hotel Otani has its own certified Santa Claus, and yes, this did make me very happy.

As it turned out, after running around shopping, checking out the castle, taking a dip in the hot tub AND the onsen and getting a miracle massage I was just in time to get back to my room and enjoy a libation (sorry, that's a cup of tea – I slipped into spa speak) as the sun set over Osaka Castle.

We then rallied for a wonderful evening enjoying the bars of the hotel (and finally getting a table at a restaurant – this was another one that proved tricky – mostly because the restaurants closed so early) and getting to bed far too late for a comfortable early morning start.

HOTEL NEW OTANI
SANTA CLAUS HOUSE

The rooms here were nice, a lot bigger than the Granvia Wakayama, although nothing more exceptional than a standard chain such as a Holiday Inn, but the body of the hotel, the facilities, the fabulous service, including calling round shops to see if they had any Godzilla toys in stock, directing me to the local department store to buy a new case and prebooking and paying for our taxi to the airport meant we got exactly what we needed and then had time for a little luxury (which we also kind of needed) – making the most of our last minutes in Japan.

Facilities: Shopping centre, official Santa Claus, 12 restaurants, bars, hair salon, onsen and fitness centre, spa, 2 chapels, dentist and medical facility.

Booked on Expedia, around £185 per room per night

The Spa and Massage – Osaka – New Hotel Otani

I wasn't sure whether a long steam and soak in my own tub would be more beneficial than the spa. (As it turned out I barely used my bathroom I spent so long here). They have a great range of facilities and will even lend you sports kit for a class. I thought I'd give the hot tub, massive pool (under a glass ceiling so you get daylight) and onsen a go. Funnily enough, although the hot tub was exceptional, it didn't hit the spot, only a hot, hot onsen was cutting it for me in Japan.

Unlike the other two onsen I'd visited, this one had a cold tub and it was busy. Luckily by now I wasn't worried about being checked out by the locals; I knew my way around a good pre-scrubbing on a Japanese bathing stool and I wasn't even put off by a little smiling and nodding as the lady next to me handed me extra washcloths. As much as my steam in Wakayama had helped, nothing beats the hot and cold of the traditional onsen to help clear whatever ails you. Actually I take that back – the massage here beat everything. The massage was in a separate spa "shop" on a different floor. I booked a little reflexology and head and scalp massage. I was still feeling incapable of much at all, but I wanted just a little more Japanese TLC (it's like… just one more type of sushi…)

Although there is very little on the hotel's website about this spa (it's such a part of their way of life that I don't think they appreciate just how awesome it is) and it's very low key with small, simple massage rooms (you can also request massages in your room), the treatments are phenomenal. I think I fell asleep a few times, I certainly heard myself snore. The pressure points she worked in my head and scalp (and perhaps my feet) did something magical in my body and by the end of the treatment I was feeling superb – no bug, no tiredness, no stress, just perfect.

Highly recommended (in fact I recommend staying at the New Hotel Otani precisely to use this spa – although I'm sure you could also do a walk-in treatment).

The Restaurant - New Otani Osaka

The New Otani Osaka has 12 restaurants (book your table early as they are busy!) We finally got a table in the evening for a long taster menu ("I love it, please make it stop") however my favourite meal was the buffet.

As you might imagine the sushi was impeccably fresh and succulent and there were many Japanese and Western delicacies. But the best treat was my visit from Father Christmas. I love Christmas, and as much as I love Japan I was looking forward to heading home and spending it with my family.

The Flight – British Airways/Finnair London Heathrow to Tokyo Narita, return from KIX (Osaka Airport, but closer to Wakayama) via Helsinki to London Heathrow

All our flights ran pretty much to time, for which I was grateful.

Strangely enough for a British Airways flight the hospitality and food were Japanese style, which was very nice as it made us feel like we were already in Japan, however on the way back as I was struggling with a bug I was desperate for some proper hot tea (I don't think this is a cultural difference as all the tea I had in Japan was lovely – this was more an airplane catering limitation).

Do try to grab some sleep on the way out as it's an overnight flight – unfortunately I couldn't, but the in-flight entertainment was vast and the direct flight from London to Tokyo was pretty fast at 11 hours 40 minutes.

I was hoping on our return through Helsinki to visit the spa which I tried on my way back from China, however we couldn't seem to find it, there was some building work going on, and in my exhausted and sick state all I had left in me was to locate another Starbucks and order a really, really hot tea.

£623.20 per person

Onsen (Japanese Hot Spring) - Etiquette and Practice

An onsen is a Japanese hot spring bath; some are located at source and others transport the water, including some hotel onsens (including Hotel Chinzanso Tokyo).

They are usually strictly naked, however most English people I have spoken to say that they have worn swimming costumes and not been kicked out. (I go naked and would advise you do the same.)

Many are single sex or have times set aside for each sex – others are mixed.

Some hotels have private onsen baths that you can reserve or which are en-suite (we had private bathrooms with onsen water at KAI Hakone but I went to the main spa because it was open air!) Many are known for the different benefits of the waters and some have famous "magical" properties.

…and some are just for animals – there is one where only monkeys relax.

They might look awkward but the little showers with stools are FANTASTIC. Japanese bathing stools are actually extremely comfortable to use. I wanted to get these for family members who have shower chairs because these are so much better; you can actually wash all around you. And it makes washing your feet so much easier.

So first of all, showering. Now I've been in many a swimming pool and spa with a big sign – "Please/You must shower before entering the pool/hot tub/whatever" and I see countless people walk past (okay, even some of my friends, with the words "Oh I had a shower this morning"). This will not cut it in Japan. There are rules you know.

Guests are expected to wash outside the shared onsen twice to avoid getting any soap, shampoo or anything else into the pure natural spring waters i.e. you wash once (properly, using the larger "towel" given, using soap and shampoo) and then once you have washed all over… do it again with just water to make completely sure that there is no soap or shampoo left on you.

You are usually given two "towels", one is for washing yourself and one you may use in the onsen. Now this is tricky because you're not supposed to get this second towel IN the onsen waters, but you can sit it on the side of the bath (having soaked it in cold water) so you can dab your face or put it on your head when you get a bit hot. (Beginners may just want to leave this alone – it's advanced bathing.)

The onsen is full of spa water, not just heated water but magic water with healing properties, so jumping in here without proper showering is like taking a beautiful white tablecloth and blowing your nose on it.

Some onsen also have a cold bath, either a small one that you can scoop water from and throw over your head and body, or a large one you can alternate with the hot waters (as at the New Hotel Otani in Osaka).

If you do get the chance to try an onsen please don't be put off by the rigmarole, once you've done it once you'll get into the habit and it is a fabulous treatment for anything that ails you, especially back pain, and as you might expect, it's great for your skin.

(I understand that some onsen do not allow people with tattoos – see The Spa – Hotel Chinzanso Tokyo. If you have tattoos you might find it easier to use a hotel onsen – in most places there was hardly anyone around when I went in and certainly no one checking to see if I had any tattoos.)

The Rest

Time Difference

9 hours ahead of London

Visa

No visa required for tourism if you have a UK passport (check the HMRC website for length of stays and up to the minute travel advice).

Language

Japanese. Most tourist areas and hotels on international websites will have many English speakers (some hotels may not appear as they cater purely to Japanese guests). Some rural areas may not (or any English signage). Be prepared to point and nod. Use your guidebook (find one that has common phrases in the back and you can just point, especially if you know you struggle with pronunciation), also have your hotel's name and the name of any sights printed out in Japanese. Also make it clear you are actually going there and not just telling your cab driver "Ooh, look, I'm staying in a nice hotel." Please don't worry, even in places where no one speaks English people are so helpful they'll make sure you're taken care of.

Vaccinations

Always check the latest recommendations from the NHS website. I have most standard vaccinations and didn't need anything else for Japan (they're more likely to need extra vaccinations coming to see us!)

Stop Bowing

Politeness is a big thing in Japan, so when you're walking down your hotel corridor and pass a hotel employee chances are that they'll bow to you, you bow back, they bow back… it could take all day. Bow, move on, or they'll never get a moment's peace.

Tipping

There is no tipping in Japan. If you leave money behind you may even cause offence. It's hard to remember, especially if you spend time in the USA - the service is so excellent that the thought kept creeping into my brain, "Oh they must expect a big tip". No, it's just that good. (Some hotels state they add a 10% service fee but it was never on our bill.)

Beautiful Presentation

If it's not beautiful, it's not finished. Give them a minute.

Currency

Japanese yen. At the time of our trip it was approximately 185¥ to £1. Yen is not the most popular currency in the UK so check ordering times. I swear by the tool on the Money Saving Expert website that gives the best rate within a certain distance (if there's nowhere close to you find the best rate and ask a local place to match it). If you preorder your currency online for the airport you'll get their best rate, but have no obligation to pick up, at the airport you'll get a much worse rate.

Cash

I found almost everywhere accepted credit cards, apart from one paper shop. It was a little tricky to take cash out of machines in Japan but bank and post office staff were very helpful. Just be aware when buying, ordering food or getting a massage you may be asked to pay in cash.

Trains and Travel Passes

I found it a nightmare researching these as there are special tourist travel and train passes you can pre-order. After all the research I found that, for us and the amount of travel we were doing, it was pretty much about the same price to buy tickets as we went along. Rail staff are very helpful, and the machines are also very efficient when it comes to buying tickets, just make sure you choose the shinkansen (bullet train) button if you're planning on using the fast service.

Getting Around

Taxis were excellent, however in order to make your life easier try to ensure you have your hotels and major destinations written in Japanese characters. You can take a screen shot of this on websites, just in case you need to ask a passer by for directions or if your taxi driver doesn't speak or read English. (They are most apologetic for not speaking English which makes me apologise even more for not speaking Japanese… and it take us ages to get anywhere.)

This can backfire as in Kyoto I showed the driver the card of the hotel and said we'd then like to go to the train station. I then realized, thanks to Google Maps that we were going the wrong way – directly to the station without our bags or you know, my client. I guess he thought I just showed him the hotel card by way of conversation, he was extremely apologetic and took too much money off the fare.

Saving Face

In the West, especially the UK, there's a lot of advice about complaining - if something is wrong with your meal or hotel or anything (or even if there's not) you make a big fuss and say you're switching in order to get a better price or service. (Unfortunately with many businesses it's the only way to get fair treatment.)

Please do not do this in Japan.

If there is a mistake as, for example, with our Kyoto taxi driver, the Japanese person will often be devastated to have inconvenienced you, there may be profuse apologies, bowing, refusal to accept money… It's quite something to witness.

This also means that when you are trying to organize something the other person may just agree without really understanding – they don't want to lose face. After our experience in Kyoto, when I organized our taxi to the Kumano Kodo our hotel receptionist, (who spoke excellent English) explained in Japanese to our elderly taxi driver. Everything seemed perfect. It was only on the road that our driver was not clear; he seemed to want to drop us off in the middle of nowhere. We finally got where we wanted to go at exactly the fee we'd agreed, but I was glued to my Google Maps the whole time checking we were actually going the right way!

Smoking

Yeah, people still smoke in a lot of places here (like Vegas) so be careful if like me you are a vehement non-smoker to double check your hotel, restaurant and bar are non-smoking. Many of the best hotels are completely non-smoking, other times you will find it in the room definition.

The only problems we had were in Hakone, when the people in the room next to me were smoking on their balcony so the smoke blew into my room through the massive windows and stank up the place while I was brushing my teeth (it doesn't take long!) In Kyoto at the local restaurant luckily we'd just finished our meal when the table next to us lit up. In Wakayama when I moved into a Japanese style room the whole floor stank of smoke (although my room was non-smoking) and in Osaka we had just found a lovely spot in a bar in our hotel when the group next to us decided to light up. Check the space is non-smoking, be prepared to close windows and be prepared to move – sadly I also had this problem in Vegas at the Bellagio with people smoking on a non-smoking floor, and when I'm sitting in a lovely park and someone sits down next to me and lights up (and in Croatia and Bosnia where I'm editing this book and smoking inside is still a thing). I guess the universe is trying to teach me to be more tolerant or get me moving – I'm working on both! (Or get me to switch my pension fund to one which has no holdings in tobacco companies – yes, I took a closer look and found I am a shareholder in several!)

Vending Machines

Yes, Japan is the home of the vending machine – everywhere. You can get a hot can of coffee out of somebody's garden on the way to Nachi Falls, cold drinks on train platforms and well, it's just awesome. There are websites devoted to listing all the things you can buy in a vending machine in Japan (I actually bumped into one selling chocolate vibrators in Salamanca, Spain.)

Toilets

After travelling through China ("it was the best of toilets, it was the worst of toilets") Japan was a revelation. It's almost worth flying here just to use their loos. Just fabulous.

In more traditional areas where you're asked to take your shoes off at the door, you'll find a pair of slippers in the toilet, you put these on just to use the loo so that the germs on the toilet floor stay on the toilet floor and you do not carry them out. It's a lot to remember in the middle of the night when you're staying in a ryokan, but what a brilliant concept (my mum fell a little bit in love with it).

There seemed to be toilets everywhere, especially in Tokyo. Some of the most wonderful were actually station toilets, it's a far cry from London and British train stations where you're lucky if a toilet is even unlocked, let alone clean and stocked with loo paper. As a Londoner I felt deeply sorry for any Japanese person visiting London, toilets must be hell for them.

The toilet technology is marvellous. (Although I'll be honest Shanghai toilets in the top hotels are on a par, or dare I say even better.) It is worth getting used to some of the symbols when you use an English "speaking" toilet, otherwise you might find yourself in Hakone desperately looking at a sparkling metal control panel with no idea how to flush (or which kind of flush is which).

My absolute favourite thing about Japanese toilets is this, when we first arrived at the Hotel Chinzanso Tokyo I thought my toilet might be broken as it seemed to run water as soon as I walked in – or perhaps it had an automatic cistern filling function, but then it flushed afterwards? All became clear in a department store toilet, which had lots of English explanations. "There is a 20 second water sound for your modesty." Yes, the Japanese toilet is so polite it plays a water noise to cover up er… any noise you might be making. How very wonderful.

Tatami Mats and Taking Shoes Off In General

Customs differ across Japan, however if there is a tatami mat chances are you're expected to take off your shoes and walk in either socks or indoor slippers (not the toilet slippers) provided. One place also asked that we not put down any dirty laundry or towels.

It never hurts to ask when entering; coffee shop, hotel, spa, even restaurants, if they would like you to take your shoes off. It's usually obvious from the rack of shoes next to the door but in a country this polite people might be too embarrassed to ask you.

Ryokans

The ryokan is a traditional inn and for me staying at KAI Hakone was one of the highlights of the trip. This is a truly luxurious experience, but having experienced for myself how clean, friendly and polite Japan is, I would have no hesitation in staying in a very simple ryokan. (Also I feel like I understand the customs enough not to make a hideous faux pas.) Many ryokans have shared bathrooms, something which put me off before, but I'd have no hesitation in sharing a bathroom with others following the ryokan customs as it would remain spotless (the only worry is other tourists…)

Surgical Face Masks

You'll often see people wearing surgical masks, especially on planes. These are to prevent them picking up anything and also more often, outside of airports and airplanes, to prevent passing on germs, especially from coughs and colds. Coughing and sneezing indiscriminately in Japan may seriously offend the locals. All shops seem to stock surgical masks (they even have cute kids' ones in pink and blue) so if you are suffering then do pick up a pack and wear one if you are coughing or sneezing – it's the done thing and very considerate of others. I wish I'd worn one before I picked up a bug, but started wearing one as soon as I started coughing. I am now disgusted when I see people coughing into their hands and touching things without thinking, it's a crazy practice when you think about it.

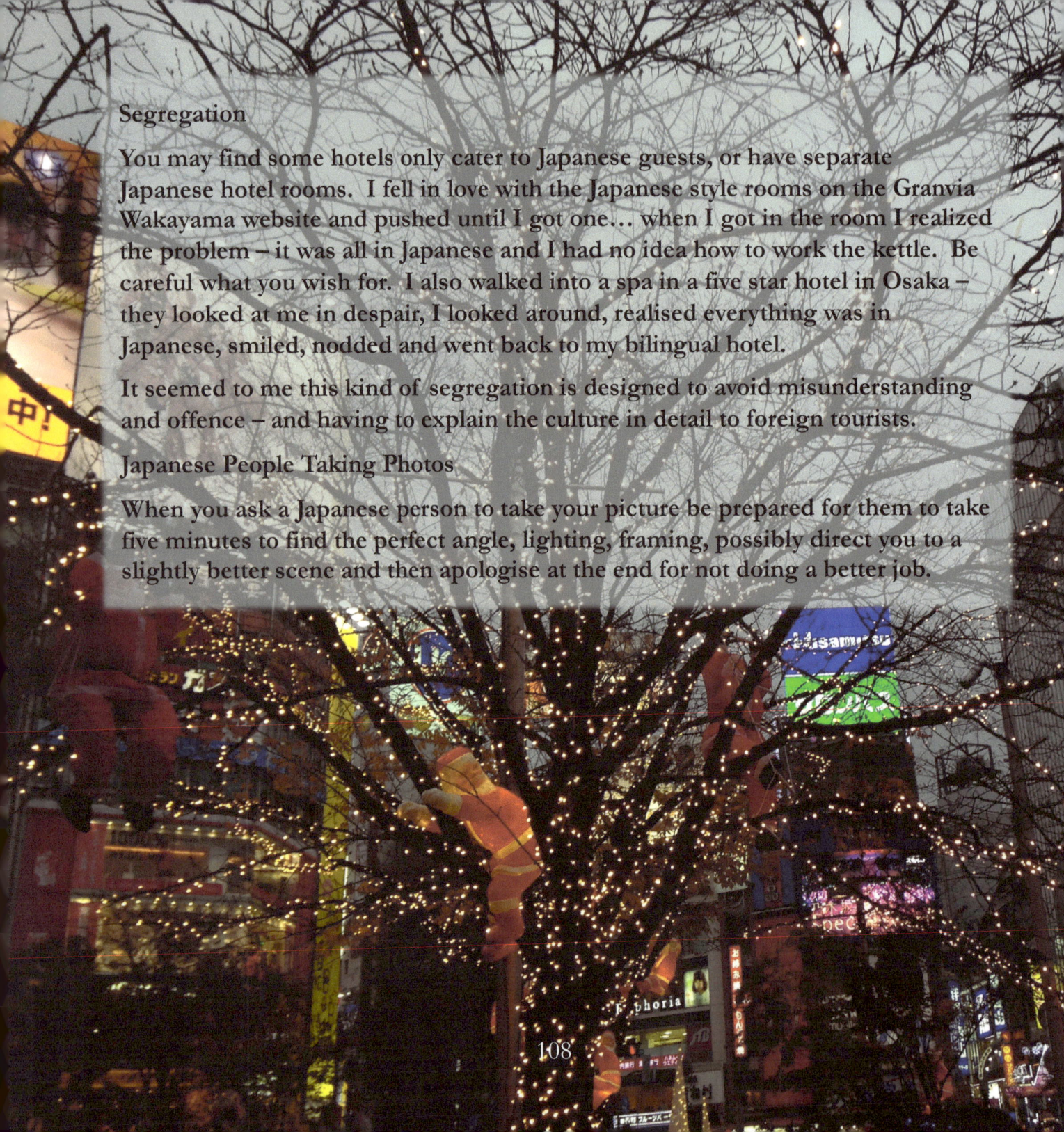

Segregation

You may find some hotels only cater to Japanese guests, or have separate Japanese hotel rooms. I fell in love with the Japanese style rooms on the Granvia Wakayama website and pushed until I got one… when I got in the room I realized the problem – it was all in Japanese and I had no idea how to work the kettle. Be careful what you wish for. I also walked into a spa in a five star hotel in Osaka – they looked at me in despair, I looked around, realised everything was in Japanese, smiled, nodded and went back to my bilingual hotel.

It seemed to me this kind of segregation is designed to avoid misunderstanding and offence – and having to explain the culture in detail to foreign tourists.

Japanese People Taking Photos

When you ask a Japanese person to take your picture be prepared for them to take five minutes to find the perfect angle, lighting, framing, possibly direct you to a slightly better scene and then apologise at the end for not doing a better job.

Photo Credits

All photos by Pearl Howie.

About the Author

For the last 8 years I've felt called to experience and write about as many escapes, particularly massage, spas and healing as I can.

I've written many books about my experiences with the hope that they will help people in some way, but I do it because I love to write, love to teach, love to share the miracles I've experienced. It also means a lot to me to help people out of pain, whether it's the torment of deciding whether to donate a kidney, supporting someone to get pain relief, helping people to understand and manage their anger. It's also wonderful to hear that just following the beat of my own drum has inspired others to follow their hearts and do astounding things. It takes the pressure off me to do things myself and just be free to hug trees and hang out in the woods.

I may be a shaman depending on what day it is and how you choose to define the word – this is my attempt from my last book; "a shaman is someone who is aware of the importance of spirituality in healing and uses that awareness to help heal mind, body and spirit."

If you'd like to know more check out my website www.pearlescapes.co.uk

Other Titles by the Author

Books in this Series

Japan Is Very Wonderful (travel)

free Feeling Real Emotions Everyday (self help)

Camino de la Luna – Take What You Need (self help/travel)

Camino de la Luna – Unconditional Love (self help/travel)

Camino de la Luna – Forgiveness (self help/travel)

Camino de la Luna – Compassion and Self Compassion (self help/travel)

Camino de la Luna – Courage (self help/travel)

Camino de la Luna – Truth (self help/travel)

Camino de la Luna – Reconciliation (self help/travel)

Other Titles

The Guide to Spa Breaks and Escapes from Pearl Escapes

The Guide to Massage, Spa Treatments and Healing from Pearl Escapes

Meditation for Angry People

The Wee, The Wound And The Worries: My Experience Of Being A Kidney Donor

Love And The Perfect Wave (romantic novel)

Individual regional guides to spas and escapes, including: Cozumel, Las Vegas, London Spas and Massage, Bath Spa, Swimming With Wild Manatees, Tuscany With Teenagers, The Lake District, Brockenhurst, Iceland, Florida, Key Largo, Orlando, Vero Beach, The Everglades, Clearwater, New York, Paris With Kids, Marrakech, China (Hong Kong, Yangshuo, Shanghai, Huangshan and Beijing), Zadar, Croatia and Barcelona

Video Everything To Dance For

www.ingramcontent.com/pod-product-compliance
Lightning Source LLC
Chambersburg PA
CBHW041124300426
44113CB00002B/46